NATIONAL AUDUBON SOCIETY POCKET GUIDE

EARTH FROM SPACE

Text by Dr. Amy Leventer and Dr. Geoffrey Seltzer
Alfred A. Knopf, New York

Contents

Introduction

How to Use This Guide

Images of Earth taken from space offer us a new perspective on our planet. In these images we can see the geologic and hydrologic action that shapes our landscape: the flowing motion of glaciers, the tectonic plate boundaries along fault lines, and the pushed-up crust along a mountain chain. Superimposed on the larger geologic structures we can also see humankind's impact on the land: rain forest devastation, reclaimed desert land, agricultural and urban subdivisions. This juxtaposition of imagery can deepen our appreciation of our planet and our understanding of our impact here.

Coverage This guide includes 80 color images of Earth, including all seven continents, that were taken from space or were compiled from data sent to Earth by space-based satellites.

Organization This easy-to-use pocket guide is divided into three parts: introductory essays, photographs of our planet from space accompanied by detailed text descriptions, and appendices.

Introduction The essay "Earth from Space" offers a brief introduction to the purposes of space-based imagery and the kinds of processes that have shaped our landscapes. "Plate Tectonics" explains how volcanoes, earthquakes, and

6

continental plates, driven by the heat within Earth's core, act upon our land surface, forming mountains, valleys, and islands. "The Hydrologic Cycle" discusses water's impact on the land, including the effects of climate and of erosion and deposition by rivers and glaciers. "Wind Effects" describes another agent that sculpts our landscape, forming dunes and carving rock formations. "Space-based Imaging" is an essay on the techniques used to generate the sorts of images found in this book. It is illustrated with 12 images of our planet made using a variety of techniques.

The Earth from Space   This section includes 80 color plates, each accompanied by a detailed description. The first seven images cover our world as a whole, oceans and seas, and the atmosphere. Then we cover each continent and various specific features within it, in the following order: North America, South America, Europe, Africa, Asia, Australia, and Antarctica. The accompanying maps pinpoint the area featured.

Appendices   Following the color plates are a world map illustrating the major tectonic plates and a detailed index.

Earth from Space

In the 1960s, Apollo astronauts brought back thrilling images of our planet, dubbed Spaceship Earth, floating in the void of space. Since then, technological advances have allowed us to develop an unprecedented perspective of our planet from space. Satellites orbit Earth equipped with instruments that measure the visible and nonvisible electromagnetic radiation from Earth's surface and atmosphere, allowing us to monitor our globe with ever-increasing clarity.

The development of the technology to produce remote images of Earth's surface from space has two implications. The first is that we can observe large-scale phenomena that are difficult if not impossible to observe from land-based measurements. For example, with various satellite technologies, we can now constantly monitor the destruction of rain forests in the tropics, the motion of glaciers in Antarctica, and the development of storms and their movements over continental regions. This allows us to monitor the pulse of change on Earth, which becomes increasingly important as the impact of humans is felt upon large-scale natural phenomena. The second advancement this technology provides is in giving us the capability to study the natural variability of different systems through continuous monitoring over broad regions. By studying year-to-year changes in climate, for example, we can begin to determine whether certain variations are part of the natural system or are caused by human interference.

Although humans can affect Earth's surface, geologic, hydrologic, and atmospheric factors control the environmental context in which anthropogenic (human-impact) activities take place. These processes are continually altering Earth's crust. The continents and oceans that exist today are only temporary features when considered on the geologic time scale.

The processes that shape Earth's surface can be divided into two broad categories: those that are internal to Earth, and those that are external. The motions of plate tectonics, which act to build mountains and create new seafloor, are of the internal type, driven by the heat trapped within Earth. The hydrologic cycle—the circulation of water through ocean, atmosphere, and land—constitutes an external process driven by energy from the Sun. These processes—internal and external—are continually sculpting and molding the surface of our Earth.

Plate Tectonics

The plate tectonic theory links such disparate geological phenomena as volcanic eruptions, earthquakes, and mountain formation, and explains how Earth's internal heat and movements have molded the planet's surface over time. Within the rotating cloud of gas and dust from which our solar system began to form some 4.6 billion years ago, material began to pull together into discrete masses. These heated up as they contracted, but only the central mass, the proto-Sun, was large enough to generate the energy needed to promote nuclear fusion. The outlying masses contracted and eventually cooled, forming the planets. As Earth cooled and its surface solidified, heat was trapped in the interior. Additional heat continues to be generated today in the interior by the decay of radioactive elements.

The high heat caused differentiation of the interior. Hot, partially molten iron forms the *core*. Lighter elements migrated to the surface, where they cooled and formed the *crust*. Between them is the *mantle*, which is partially molten because of the heat generated in the core and the pressure of the overlying crust. Geologists believe that the heat trapped within Earth moves the crust and the upper portion of the mantle—collectively referred to as

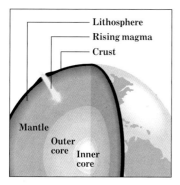

Lithosphere

Rising magma

Crust

Mantle

Outer core

Inner core

the *lithosphere*—through convection currents (circulatory heat transfer) in the mantle. The lithosphere is broken into approximately a dozen rigid *tectonic plates,* which are constantly moving as a result of these convection currents. Relative motion between the plates occurs at a rate of about 2 to 17 cm (1 to 7 inches) per year. The map on page 187 illustrates Earth's major tectonic plates.

There are three types of motion along the boundaries of these plates: divergent, convergent, and transform motions. At *divergent boundaries* the plates are moving away from each other, and magma rises from below the lithosphere and fills the void that is created, thus forming new crust. Such activity is occurring today along the mid-ocean ridges, such as the Mid-Atlantic Ridge. It is also responsible for the Great Rift Valley in Africa, which formed when crustal blocks separated and dropped relative to the adjoining continent, and magma rose and solidified in the voids between these blocks.

At *convergent boundaries,* two plates are colliding. All the major mountain belts and 80 percent of the volcanoes on Earth are located along convergent plate boundaries. Mountains are created by the compressional forces

11

between converging plates and by magma rising from the mantle. Magma is generated along those convergent plate boundaries where one plate is subducted beneath another. Under these conditions, partial melting results in the production of magma. If the magma erupts at the surface it forms volcanoes. Most active volcanoes are found along convergent plate boundaries, such as the one in the Andes where the Nazca Plate is being subducted beneath the South American Plate. However, some volcanoes form within plates, such as the Hawaiian Islands, which are believed to have formed over a relatively stationary hot spot—where magma rises from deep within the mantle— beneath the Pacific Plate. As the Pacific Plate inches along, the magma has built up the Hawaiian chain. To this day, new land is being formed on the Big Island of Hawaii.

Transform boundaries occur where tectonic plates are sliding by one another. This is occurring today along California's San Andreas Fault, where the Pacific Plate is moving by the North American Plate. Stop-and-go motion produces earthquakes along the fault line.

The Hydrologic Cycle

Water is one of the dominant external agents responsible for shaping Earth's surface. It is critical for life, and its availability affects the wide variety of vegetation on our planet. Flowing in rivers or inching along as glacial ice, water provides an important agent for erosion and deposition. It also causes the weathering of bedrock, which leads to the formation of soils, causes landslides, and dissolves limestone to produce caves.

The hydrologic cycle describes the movement of water on Earth. Water is stored in various reservoirs, including the oceans, glaciers, groundwater, lakes, rivers, and the atmosphere. It is transferred among these reservoirs by processes such as melting, evaporation, precipitation, and the natural flow caused by gravity.

The Sun provides the energy necessary to drive the hydrologic cycle. The evaporation of water from the oceans produces most of the precipitation over land. This precipitation moves through the hydrologic cycle by various pathways, including groundwater and rivers, before eventually returning to the ocean. Without the Sun to drive the initial evaporation of water from the oceans, the hydrologic cycle would lie dormant.

Circulation in the oceans and the atmosphere redistributes the solar energy received at Earth's surface. A relative excess of energy is received in tropical latitudes. In the oceans, warm surface currents generated in the low latitudes, such as the Gulf Stream in the Atlantic Ocean, act to distribute excess energy in the oceans to higher latitudes. Cold water from the polar regions is returned toward the equator by deep currents that upwell along the western boundaries of the continents. For instance, the cold Peruvian (or Humboldt) Current originates around the Antarctic continent and flows northward, upwelling along the western coast of South America. The Pacific coast of northern Chile and Peru is extremely dry (the cold air underlying warm air higher in the atmosphere prevents cloud formation) and relatively cool all year because of the presence the Peruvian Current offshore.

In the atmosphere, warm air in the tropics moves toward higher latitudes, where it eventually sinks, producing zones of high pressure at about 30° N and S latitudes. Located in these zones of descending air are some of the driest regions on Earth, including Africa's major deserts, the Sahara and the Kalahari. Interactions between warm air moving toward higher latitudes and cold air returning from the polar regions generates storms at middle latitudes. These storms are carried along by the prevailing westerly winds, which produce rain forests in coastal regions such as southeastern Alaska. Differential solar heating of land and ocean surfaces can also result in seasonal periods of high rainfall, such as the Asian monsoons.

Rivers Many of the landforms featured in this book were molded by rivers acting on the geologic substrate. Although rivers comprise only a small volume of the water on Earth, water moves quickly through them, making them major agents of erosion. Rivers can erode the landscape by abrading the underlying bedrock and by entraining the loose sediment in their flow. The erosive ability of a river depends on its gradient, the volume of water it carries, and the resistance of the underlying bedrock. Generally rivers on steep mountain slopes have many channels, often with a braided appearance, whereas rivers crossing flatter regions have a sinuous or meandering appearance. Rivers form drainage networks, which are the systems of channels that drain a region. The Colorado River, which flows through the Grand Canyon, has a drainage network of associated rivers that encompasses an area of nearly 630,000 sq km (245,000 sq mi).

Rivers deposit large accumulations of sediment in lakes and oceans at their mouths. The slowing down of the river water as it enters a relatively still body of water causes the sediment to drop. Deltas are constantly growing, and the channels that feed them shift back and forth. Rivers not only move about 9 billion tons of sediment from their headwaters to the oceans annually, they also carry about 4 billion tons of dissolved materials as a result of chemical weathering processes on the landscape. Thus rivers are an important factor in shaping the surface of the continents as they continually wear down the topographic relief produced by tectonic forces. The Grand Canyon is a feature formed by erosion, mainly by the Colorado River. The Nile Delta is a landmass built by deposition of sediment carried by the river.

Glaciers
Over the last 2 million years, there have been many periods when large glaciers covered the North American and Eurasian continents, and smaller glaciers occupied alpine valleys. The repeated growth and decay of glaciers has resulted in the landscapes with which many of us are

familiar, especially in mountainous areas and at higher latitudes. In regions where snow accumulation outstrips snowmelt, such as the Antarctic continent, glaciers form as excess snow becomes buried year after year and eventually compresses into ice. Once the ice becomes thick enough, it begins to flow under the influence of gravity. As the base of a glacier moves over the landscape it scours the underlying rock, entraining debris in its ice. This debris can enhance the capacity of the glacier to erode its bed. The U-shaped valleys in mountainous areas, such as the Yosemite Valley in California, form as valleys are widened and deepened by the action of glaciers and their debris. *Fjords* form in coastal areas as glaciers erode land below the level of the sea, as in Glacier Bay, Alaska. At the ends of glaciers, rock debris melts out of the ice, often forming chaotic deposits called *moraines,* such as the moraine that forms Cape Cod. Rock debris and melted glacier ice are also carried away by rivers, resulting in large river valleys filled with thick deposits of gravel, as can be observed along the Mississippi River.

Wind Effects

The wind is also a significant agent in sculpting the landscape. The major features we observe that are produced by wind are dunes. Dunes form in environments where there is sufficient fine-grained material, such as sand and silt, and consistent winds that can mobilize this material. Hence dunes can form along the coasts of oceans and large lakes, along floodplains of large rivers in arid regions, and in deserts. Where there is insufficient sand to form dunes, the prevailing winds can winnow out all the finer-grained material, leaving behind deposits of gravel called *desert pavement*. If a significant amount of sand is caught up in the wind, the result can be a sand-blasting action that forms *ventifacts*, or rocks sculpted by the wind. When dunes form, they take on characteristic shapes that are indicative of the quantity of sand and silt available and the strength and direction of the prevailing winds. *Barchan dunes* are crescent-shaped, with their ends pointed downwind. In regions with abundant sand, *transverse dunes* can form; these are ridges of sand that lie at right angles to the direction of the prevailing winds. Dunes are not stationary features on the landscape; they migrate as their upwind sides erode and sand accumulates along their lee sides.

Space-based Imaging

Space-based observation of Earth provides exciting evidence of the dynamics of our atmosphere, oceans, and the continents. The uses of air- and space-based imagery include: surveying land; predicting weather and tracking storms; monitoring crops, deforestation, soil erosion, droughts, and floods; locating oil and mineral resources; tracking ocean circulatory patterns; urban planning; intelligence gathering and reconnaissance; assessing disasters; topographical mapping; and locating ancient archaeological sites. In addition to the practical uses of satellite images of Earth, there is real social value in being able to monitor large-scale phenomena in order to detect changes induced by human activity and to establish the natural variability of various systems.

Imaging Techniques

Space-based images of Earth range from the images taken by astronauts with hand-held cameras to computer-generated mosaics compiled from the data of thousands of satellite images. Satellites operate on various imaging systems that are sensitive to different wavelengths in the electromagnetic spectrum, such as visible light, infrared light, and radio waves. Radiation from the Sun reflects off terrestrial surfaces in the visible-light range of the

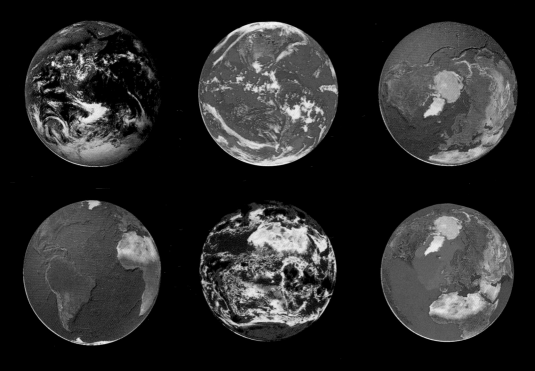

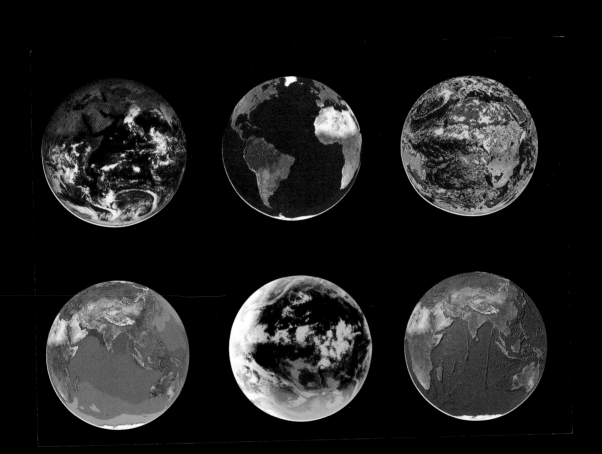

electromagnetic spectrum, which can be recorded by conventional photographic means. The sensors in satellites can observe the nonvisible portion of the electromagnetic spectrum. Some satellites record data with radar, which detects radio waves. Radar's advantages over visible-light methods are that it can penetrate cloud cover and sand (revealing the rock and even ancient roadways underneath) and that it can be used day or night.

Many of the images in this book were made with data recorded by the Landsat satellites. The Landsat program was introduced by the U.S. National Aeronautics and Space Administration in 1975. The Landsat satellites observe the visible to thermal-infrared portion of the electromagnetic spectrum. When these images are compiled from digital information sent to Earth by the Landsat satellites, different portions of the electromagnetic spectrum are assigned different colors. Red usually denotes vegetation, and blue indicates urban build-up.

The globes on pages 20–21 are the results of various imaging techniques. The top left globe on page 20 is a visible-light photograph of our planet from space. The three topographical globes (page 20, top right and bottom left; page 21, bottom right) showing the features of Earth's crust were computer generated by the GeoSphere Project, with land-cover data from satellites and ocean topography information from the U.S. Geological Survey. Thousands of images from National Oceanic and Atmospheric Administration satellites were compiled by the GeoSphere Project to make the natural-looking views of our planet (some with ocean temperatures illustrated in different gradients of blue) at top center and bottom right on page 20, and at top center and bottom left on page 21. The false-color globe on the top-left of page 21 highlights weather patterns. The two brightly colored globes are images from Meteosat, which detects infrared radiation (heat). The image of Earth's nightside, with a thin crescent of daylight showing (page 21, bottom center), was also taken by Meteosat.

The images throughout this book range from photographs taken by space shuttle astronauts to weather satellite composites to computer-generated mosaics compiled from thousands of satellite images.

EARTH FROM SPACE

World Topography

Earth's topographical face is the result of millions of years of plate tectonics, seafloor spreading, and continental drift, all of which caused the ancient supercontinent Pangaea to break up into the seven individual continents that constitute our world today: North America, South America, Africa, Europe, Asia, Antarctica, and Australia. The colors in this topographical map depict heights above or below the geoid, a surface of constant gravity that approximates sea level. The darkest blue represents deep ocean. Trenches, which mark collisional tectonic plate boundaries in the oceans, are visible as the curved dark lines in the ocean basins and are especially common in the Pacific. Mid-ocean ridges, such as the one running like a zipper through the Atlantic, are sites of seafloor spreading, where new oceanic crust is being formed by undersea volcanism. Lighter blue shows the continental shelves, extensions of the continents that are submerged under today's high sea level but were emergent when sea level was lower, as during the height of the last major glaciation, 18,000 years ago. Orange represents land currently above sea level, and dark orange indicates elevated regions, such as mountain ranges and high plateaus.

Ocean Floors

Landmasses comprise only 30 percent of Earth's surface. Water, mainly in the form of oceans, covers the remaining 70 percent. This computer-generated view highlights many of the tectonic features of our ocean floors. The Pacific Basin is outlined by deep trenches, areas where tectonic plates collide, with one plate subducted beneath the other. Such collisions cause intense earthquake and volcanic activity, which often gives rise to seismic sea waves, or tsunamis. The trenches of the Japanese and Aleutian island chains are sites of recent tectonic activity. The deepest site on Earth, the Challenger Deep (11,022 m/ 36,152 feet below sea level), is located just south of Japan in the Mariana Trench. The L-shaped line in the north-central Pacific marks the Hawaiian Island–Emperor Seamount chain, a series of volcanic islands that has formed as the Pacific plate moves over a hot spot deep in Earth's interior. These mantle plumes periodically force magma (molten rock) to Earth's surface, where the extruded lava forms or adds to volcanic islands. The Big Island of Hawaii is currently over the hot spot and has one of the most active volcanoes on Earth.

28

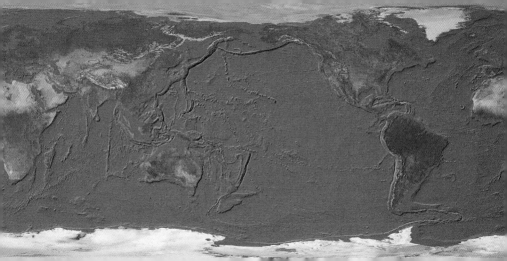

Global Ocean Temperatures

This image is a mosaic composed of data collected by National Oceanic and Atmospheric Administration (NOAA) weather satellites. Individual images were selected for this composite based on absence of cloud cover and good representation of surface land coloration. Sea-ice cover in the Arctic and glacial and sea-ice cover in the Antarctic can be seen at the top and bottom of the image, respectively. The pink tinge represents tundra, most common in the subpolar areas. Vegetated regions appear green; arid areas are yellow. The shades of blue in the oceans represent gradations in temperature, with darkest blue indicating warmest waters, and lighter blues progressively colder ones. Isotherms, or lines of constant temperature, are oriented roughly east-west, except where they are distorted by currents and by persistent upwelling. For example, the northward travel of cold Antarctic water toward Africa along the Benguela Current can be seen. Upwelling of cold water occurs along the western boundary of many continents. These are sites of extremely high primary production, and significant fisheries are often associated with them.

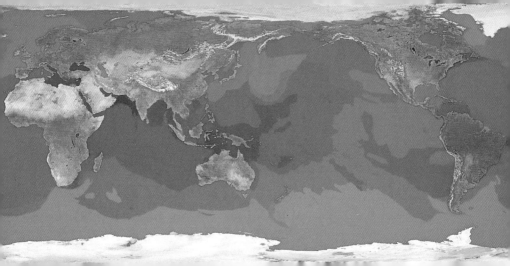

Global Surface Temperatures

This image displays global average surface temperatures in January 1979. The distribution of temperatures is as follows: purple = −38°C (−36°F); blue = −36 to −12°C (−33 to 10°F); green = −10 to 0°C (14 to 32°F); yellow = 2 to 14°C (36 to 57°F); pink, orange, and red = 16 to 34°C (59 to 93°F); deep red and black = 36 to 40°C (95 to 104°F). The excess of heat energy in low latitudes (near the equator) and the deficit in the polar regions result primarily from the angle of incoming sunlight: more direct at the equator, more oblique near the poles. This unequal distribution of heat energy, along with Earth's rotation, is what drives both oceanic and atmospheric circulation. The prevailing wind systems are a direct result of the uneven heating of Earth; the winds in turn drive surface circulation of the oceans. The tilt of Earth on its axis causes the seasons. This map represents winter in the Northern Hemisphere, which is tilted away from the Sun, and summer in the Southern Hemisphere, which is tilted toward the Sun.

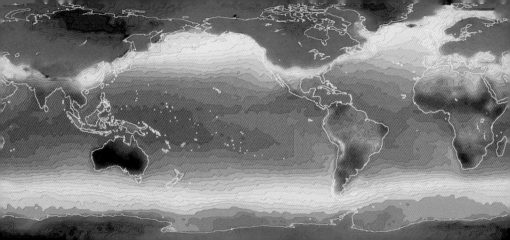

Mediterranean Sea: Phytoplankton Levels

The focus of early Western civilization, the Mediterranean is an inland sea enclosed by Europe, Africa, and Asia. Covering some 2,512,300 sq km (970,000 sq mi) and reaching a maximum depth of 5,150 m (16,896 feet), it has many smaller subdivisions, including the Adriatic, Aegean, Tyrrhenian, Ionian, and Ligurian seas. Its islands include Sicily, Sardinia, Corsica, Crete, and Malta. It is connected to the Atlantic by the Strait of Gibraltar, and to the Red Sea (lower right) and the Black Sea (upper right) by the Suez Canal and the Dardanelles/Marmara/ Bosporus waterway, respectively. This image represents phytoplankton concentrations in surface waters, with highest concentrations shown in red, and progressively decreasing densities in orange, yellow, green, and blue (lowest). Extremely high levels are obvious in the Atlantic Ocean north and west of Spain and in the Black Sea. Low densities occur throughout most of the Mediterranean. Phytoplankton, microscopic plantlife, are an essential element in the food chain. Images such as this, which help pinpoint areas of high nutrient content with plentiful fish, can indicate pollution and other problems.

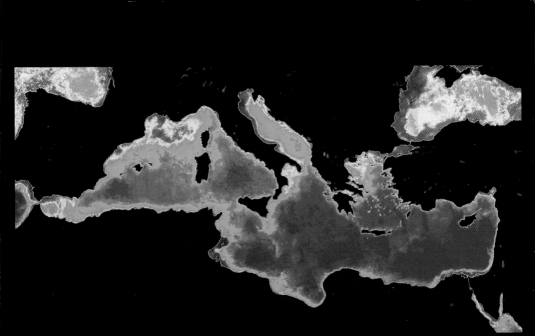

Hurricane Iniki

Hurricane Iniki hit the coastline of the Hawaiian island of Kauai on September 11, 1992. At its strongest, Iniki generated winds at speeds exceeding 240 km/hour (149 mph) and generated waves more than 5 m (16 feet) high. Hurricanes and tropical storms develop when warm, evaporating water from the equatorial ocean removes heat from the water and produces a band of low pressure at the equator. Near the end of summer, intense low-pressure cells break away from the equatorial low-pressure belt and move toward higher latitudes as tropical storms that can develop into hurricanes if they gather enough heat energy. A tropical storm reaches hurricane status when its wind speeds exceed 119 km/hour (74 mph). After striking Kauai, this storm weakened and was downgraded to a tropical storm as it moved over the cooler waters of the North Pacific (as pictured here). The absence of thunderstorm activity at the center of this swirling cloud mass is evidence of this weakening. This photograph was taken by the crew of the space shuttle *Endeavour*.

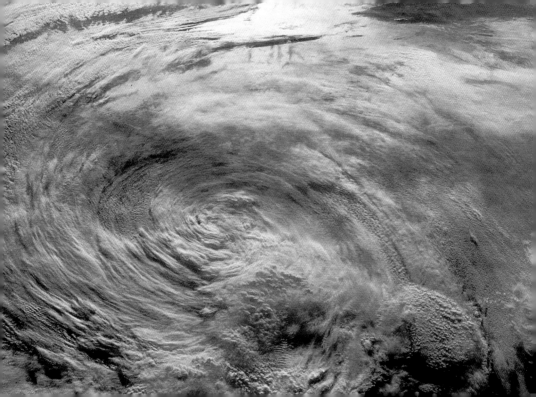

Auroras

The aurora australis, or southern lights, are seen in
this space shuttle photograph. The northern lights
are termed aurora borealis. Auroras are a luminous
phenomenon of the upper atmosphere, seen primarily
in the arctic latitudes of both hemispheres. They occur
when charged particles ejected from the Sun by way of
solar flares and solar wind arrive in the vicinity of Earth
and are captured by our magnetic field and conducted
downward toward the magnetic poles. These electrons
and protons interact with atoms of oxygen and nitrogen
in the upper atmosphere, knocking electrons away and
leaving charged ions behind. These ions emit radiation,
which creates the characteristic red and greenish-blue
colors of an aurora. During periods of intense solar
activity, auroras can sometimes be seen in middle
latitudes as close to the equator as 30° latitude.
Auroras take many forms, including arcs, bands,
patches, and curtains.

North America

The third-largest continent, covering about 24,350,000 sq km (9,400,000 sq mi), North America includes all lands in the Western Hemisphere north of the Isthmus of Panama, including Canada, the United States, Mexico, Central America, Hawaii, the West Indies, and Greenland. Its altitude ranges from 86 m (282 feet) below sea level at Death Valley, California, to 6,194 m (20,316 feet) at Denali (Mount McKinley), Alaska. This image shows the continent's major physiographic and biogeographic provinces. Permanent ice cover appears white. The boreal forest, consisting of coniferous vegetation, extends in a dark green band from the Canadian Rockies in the west to the Great Lakes in the east. North of the boreal forest is the Arctic tundra (brown), a treeless region with intensely cold winters and a brief growing season. South of the boreal forest are the high deserts of the western United States and Mexico (mottled-brown), the prairies of the midwest (brown and green), and the green forests, pastures, and wetlands of the east. Tropical vegetation is found in southern Florida, southern Mexico, and Central America (not shown here).

40

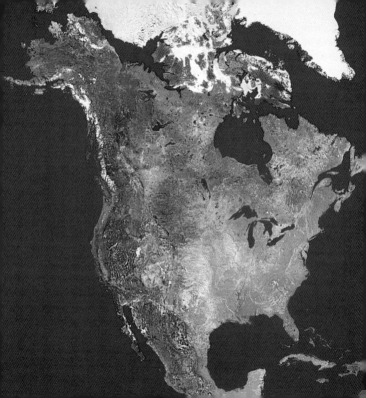

Columbia River Area

The Columbia River, which bisects this image, forms the border between Washington and Oregon before it empties into the Pacific Ocean. Its mouth is the only deep-water harbor between San Francisco and Cape Flattery, Washington, and the river is navigable by seagoing boats for 152 km (95 miles). Portland, Oregon, is located at a bend in the river at its junction with the Willamette River, below and right of center in this image. The Portland metropolitan area extends to the south in the Willamette Valley. Vancouver, Washington, is just across the Columbia River to the north. To the west are the Coast Ranges, which extend from southern California to Alaska, an area of frequent rainfall covered by dense stands of Douglas fir and hemlock. The Pacific coastline is abrupt, with dramatic seawalls, narrow beaches, and sea stacks, which are columns of rock protruding offshore. Once part of the mainland, sea stacks remain when erosion weathers away weaker surrounding rock. On the right-hand (eastern) side of this image is the Cascade Range. Mount St. Helens, which erupted in 1980 after lying dormant for 120 years, is clearly visible.

San Francisco Bay Area

This Landsat image of the San Francisco Bay area of California shows the major population centers of the region, including San Francisco, the west coast's largest port, at the top of the peninsula on the left; Oakland, directly across the bay (to the right); and San Jose, at the end of the bay in the bottom right. Four bridges can be identified: the Golden Gate Bridge, named for the 3-km (2-mile) wide strait that crosses the mouth of the bay in the upper left; the Bay Bridge, which crosses the bay from San Francisco to Oakland; the San Mateo Bridge, in the center of the image; and the Dumbarton Bridge, at the southern end of the bay. The two reservoirs south of San Francisco are located along the San Andreas Fault, part of a 960-km (600-mile) long network of faults that extends northward from the Gulf of California. Formed by two crustal plates moving past each other, these faults bring 10,000 earthquakes—mostly minor ones—to the area each year. The San Francisco Bay area had major earthquakes in 1906 and 1989, the former setting off fires that destroyed a large part of the city.

44

Hawaii: The Big Island

The island of Hawaii, known as the Big Island, is the largest, youngest, southeasternmost island in the chain. This image is oriented toward the northeast. Mauna Loa volcano (lower center), reaches 4,170 m (13,678 feet) above sea level. Measured from the seafloor, it is the most massive mountain on the planet. The dark radial pattern around the central vent is formed by lava flows and volcanic ash. Kilauea Crater, just to the east of Mauna Loa, is the most active volcano on the island. Mauna Kea (4,205 m/13,796 feet above sea level), near the top center, last erupted in 1801. Most of the island's towns are located along the coast. The generally clear, dark conditions over the center of Hawaii, unpolluted by city lights, make it an ideal location for astronomical observatories. Like the other Hawaiian Islands, the Big Island has a wet, windward (east) coast, characterized by plentiful rain and lush, tropical vegetation, and a dry leeward coast. The topography on the islands is dominated by the central volcanic peaks. Instead of north, south, east, and west, locals use two terms for directions: *makai,* toward the sea, and *mauka,* toward the mountains.

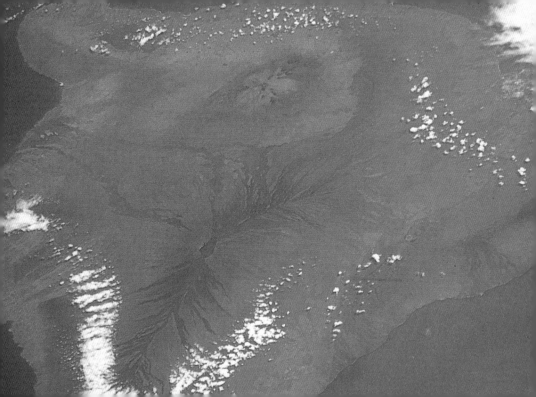

Grand Canyon and Colorado River

The Colorado River began to incise the Grand Canyon in northwestern Arizona shortly after the uplifting of the Colorado Plateau 6 million years ago. As the river erodes the rock, it carries the sediment along with it, contributing to further erosion. The walls of the canyon are eroded by rain and sand washing down the sides. The average depth of the canyon is about 1.6 km (1 mile); it measures 6 to 30 km (4 to 18 miles) from rim to rim; and it is 349 km (216 miles) long. Exposed in the canyon are sandstones, limestones, and shales, which overlie metamorphic schists, gneisses, and granite that are more than 2.5 billion years old. The Colorado River flows into Lake Mead, which is visible in the left-hand (western) portion of the image. The discharge in the river is controlled by the Glen Canyon Dam, located to the northeast on the southern end of Lake Powell (not visible in the image). In this photograph, the river and canyon snake across the image from the upper right-hand corner down to bottom center, then up to Lake Mead.

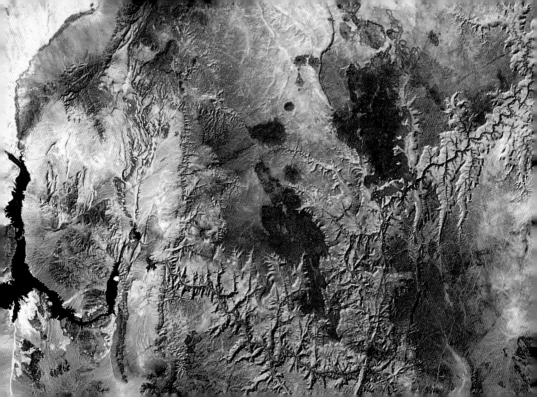

Mississippi River

The largest river in the United States, the Mississippi flows 3,780 km (2,350 miles) from Minnesota to the Gulf of Mexico. This infrared image shows old patterns on a stretch of the river. Oxbow lakes are common in the Mississippi, forming when the river changes course and old channels are cut off from the main flow. The channels migrate laterally as the outer bank of the river is eroded and gravel is deposited along the inner bank of the curve or meander. Occasionally the river cuts through the meander, and oxbow lakes form in the abandoned channels. This image shows a number of oxbow lakes that have formed in the Mississippi River bottom, as well as dry sections of old river channels. Healthy vegetation appears in red. The seasonal flooding of the river bottom has produced a fertile plain well suited for agriculture, as can be seen by the numerous fields that border the river. The constant shifting of the river produces problems in managing the floodplain and in some cases makes the clear delineation of legal boundaries difficult.

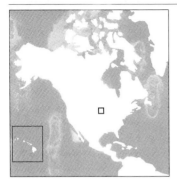

St. Louis, Missouri: Before and During 1993 Floods

These are Landsat images of the St. Louis, Missouri, area before and during the 1993 floods. The image on the left was obtained on July 4, 1988, a drought year; the image on the right was obtained on July 18, 1993, during the height of a period of extremely heavy rains that persisted for nearly two months. St. Louis is the purple area in the images, located to the lower right. Three rivers converge here: the Mississippi River flows from upper left; the Missouri River flows from bottom left, joining the Mississippi just north of the city; and the Illinois River flows from near the top center. The Mississippi continues south from the city. Above-average precipitation produced extensive flooding and damage during the summer months of 1993 in the Mississippi River drainage basin. On August 1, 1993, the flood crested in St. Louis at a record 15 m (49.4 feet), about .75 m (2.5 feet) below the top of the floodwall. Portions of southern St. Louis were flooded, but the central part of the city was spared.

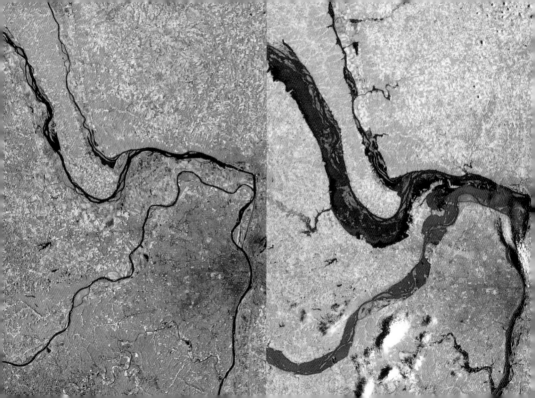

Montreal, Quebec

Canada's largest city and chief port, Montreal is in
southern Quebec, near the Ontario and New York State
borders. Named for Mount Royal, the hill at the center,
this French-Canadian city sits on the west bank of the
St. Lawrence River, which flows from bottom left to the top
right of this Landsat image. The city occupies the larger
of the two oblong islands at the center. The patchwork of
strips surrounding the city is agricultural fields (a French-
style land pattern, in contrast to the block-type English
and American subdivisions), and the V-shaped pattern
to the west is Mirabel Airport. The Ottawa River, coming
from the west, joins the St. Lawrence just south of
Montreal. The St. Lawrence continues southwestward,
through Lake St. Francis (bottom left) and Lake St. Louis,
into the St. Lawrence Seaway, which was constructed in
the 1950s to enable oceangoing ships to sail from the
Atlantic Ocean to the Great Lakes. Originating in Lake
Ontario, the St. Lawrence flows 1,216 km (760 miles)
to the Gulf of St. Lawrence. At its mouth it is 144 km
(90 miles) wide.

Florida and the Keys

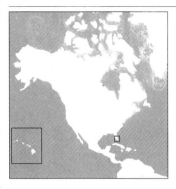

The southernmost land of the continental United States, the peninsula of Florida juts out into the Atlantic Ocean and the Gulf of Mexico. The entire state is of very low elevation, with the highest point only 105 m (345 feet) above sea level. This image shows the southern part of the state, including the Keys, a chain of islands built up on coral reefs extending southwestward off the tip. The Keys are linked to the mainland by the bridges and causeways of the Overseas Highway. Lake Okeechobee, located about three-quarters of the way down the peninsula on the east, is a freshwater lake, the largest lake in Florida. At its southern end is an agricultural area that borders on the northern end of the Everglades, a low-lying marshland with a maximum elevation of only 2 m (7 feet). The natural direction of flow in the Everglades, an area of about 12,500 sq km (5,000 sq mi) extending to the Gulf coast, is from northeast to southwest. The prominent offshore bar along the Atlantic Coast is Cape Canaveral, site of the John F. Kennedy Space Center. Just west of this area are a number of lakes formed by water filling sinkholes in this limestone-karst terrain.

New York Metropolitan Area

Once a humble trading post, New York City became the country's major shipping and financial center because of its extensive harbor and its later link to the Great Lakes via the Hudson River and the Erie Canal (built in 1825). The city's location on the Atlantic made it a natural entryway for millions of immigrants. Comprised of five boroughs, New York City appears in blue at the center of this Landsat image. Manhattan Island is circumscribed by the Hudson River on the west, which separates it from New Jersey, and the East and Harlem rivers on the east and north, which separate it from Brooklyn, Queens, and the Bronx. The Hudson River, which begins 500 km (300 miles) to the north in the Adirondacks, flows south through Upper New York Bay, the Narrows, and Lower New York Bay to the Atlantic. The large island that forms the western shore of the bays at lower left is Staten Island. Long Island extends to the east for 189 km (118 miles). Along its south shore are (west to east) Jamaica Bay, with John F. Kennedy International Airport on its eastern shore, and a string of barrier beaches: the Rockaways, Long Beach, and Jones Beach. To its north is Long Island Sound.

Cape Cod and Eastern Massachusetts

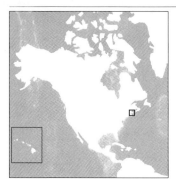

This Landsat image includes part of Boston and Boston Harbor (upper left), Providence, Rhode Island, and Narragansett Bay (lower left), and the Massachusetts shoreline in between. Cape Cod, curving 105 km (65 miles) into the ocean, and its attendant islands formed as a series of glacial moraines on the coastal plain more than 10,000 years ago, when large continental glaciers covered most of North America. Glacial moraines are ridges of rock debris that are deposited at the edge of glaciers. The hook shape and recurved spit at the end of the cape were produced by reworking of the glacial debris by ocean currents. The curving arm, from 1.6 to 32 km (1 to 20 miles) wide, encloses Cape Cod Bay. Off the southwestern part of the cape, the Elizabeth Islands enclose Buzzards Bay, which is linked to Cape Cod Bay by the 13-km (8-mile) long Cape Cod Canal, constructed in 1914 to enable ships to pass more easily to and from Boston Harbor. Just southeast of the Elizabeth chain is Martha's Vineyard, and farther east is Nantucket Island, enclosing Nantucket Sound.

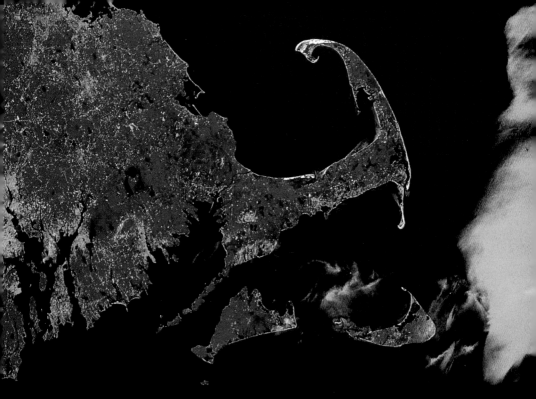

United States: City Lights

This nighttime image of the city lights of the United States provides an indication of the population densities of different regions. Cities with large surrounding metropolitan areas glow most brightly, while areas of low population density, such as the area west of the Rockies, appear dark. The brightest lights extend along the eastern seaboard from Washington, D.C., north to Boston. This is the most densely populated area of the country. The Great Lakes area is also brightly illuminated. The Chicago metropolitan area helps clearly define the southern edge of Lake Michigan. Lakes Erie and Ontario, lit by Detroit, Toronto, and Montreal, can be identified to the northeast. Florida is clearly identified by the lights from cities rimming the Atlantic and Gulf coasts. The city lights of the San Francisco Bay area and Los Angeles help to define the west coast. Farther north, Portland, Oregon, and Vancouver and Seattle, Washington, brighten the Pacific Northwest. This image was compiled from data gathered by the Defense Meteorological Satellite Program 825 km (512 miles) above Earth. These satellites are used to provide accurate weather forecasts, primarily for the military.

South America

Connected to North America by the Isthmus of Panama, South America has a wide variety of landscapes— from wet, tropical forest to desert, from glacier-topped mountains to hot, dry prairies—created by varying climatic and geologic conditions. Covering an area of 17,821,030 sq km (6,880,706 sq mi), it extends from the tropical Caribbean to the icy waters off Tierra del Fuego and Cape Horn at the southern tip. The Andes mountains run 7,200 km (4,500 miles) along the western length of the continent. Many mountain peaks in the tropical Andes top 6,000 m (19,680 feet) and are covered by small glaciers. The Amazon River and its tributaries form a dendritic (branching) pattern in the top third of the continent, the large green area in this image. The Amazon drainage basin stretches from the crest of the Andes on the west to the Atlantic Ocean on the east, passing through the world's largest rain forest. The grassy plains of Argentina and Uruguay, known as the pampas, are located between the southern Andes and the Atlantic Ocean.

Iguaçú Falls Area

The Iguaçú River flows east to west in southern Brazil, forming for a small part of its length the Brazil-Argentina border before it meets the north-south flowing Paraná River. Paraguay comprises the far left side of this image, west of the Paraná; Brazil is above the curving Iguaçú, on the right side, and Argentina is below it. The famous Iguaçú Falls are located near the center of this image where the Iguaçú River narrows. The waterfalls have a mean annual flow of about 1,708 cubic meters per second (61,000 cubic feet per second) or approximately one-third that of Niagara Falls. About 4 km (2.5 miles) wide, they include hundreds of cascades dropping as far as 70 m (230 feet) off the Paraná plateau to the gorge below. The striking change in terrain just north of the Iguaçú River marks the break between the natural vegetation in the Iguaçú National Park and agricultural activities in southern Brazil. Near the center of the image is a light green clearing with a red (soil) strip, which is the local airport. The large reservoir on the Paraná River (top right) was formed by the 1982 Itaipu Dam.

Amazon and Río Negro Confluence

Although the Nile is the world's longest river, the Amazon is the largest by volume, carrying one-fifth of the world's river water. It starts high in the Andes and flows eastward across South America, fed by hundreds of tributaries along the way. The Río Negro is the last major tributary to join the Amazon from the north on its course to the Atlantic. The Río Negro emanates from Colombia and is linked by the Casiquiare Canal, a natural channel, to the Orinoco River, which flows into the Caribbean. Manaus, located on the northern side of the confluence of the Río Negro and Amazon, is one of the few population centers in this low-lying rain forest. Manaus is 1,600 km (992 miles) from the Atlantic Ocean, yet it is only 45 m (148 feet) above sea level. Established in the 17th century as a Portuguese mission and garrison, it was the site of a rubber boom from the 1850s until World War I and now is a free-trade zone. As this false-color image shows, the sediment-heavy waters of the Amazon, represented here in blue, do not immediately mix with the clearer waters of the Río Negro, shown in black.

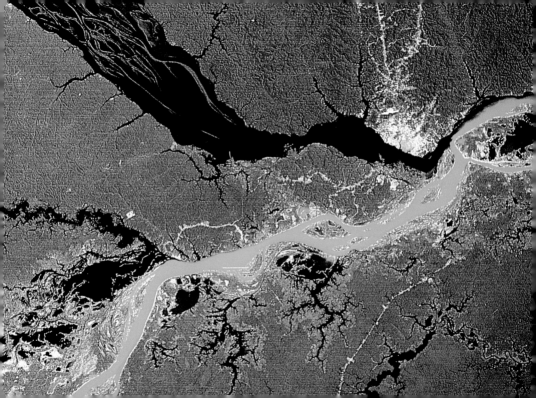

Brazil: Deforestation

This Landsat image shows deforestation in Brazil's rain forest. The linear patterns of pale green and pink, which are cuts into the forest off the main road, are the areas that have been deforested. These cleared areas contrast with the dark green of the natural forests. As people move into the tropical rain forests and clear land for agricultural, ranching, logging, and mining purposes, a number of environmental concerns arise. One concern focuses on the loss of the tropical rain forest as a major sink for atmospheric carbon dioxide and on the impact that clearing and burning the forests will have on future global warming because of an enhanced greenhouse effect. Another concern is the loss of plant and animal species. Rain forests are thought to contain nearly half the world's plant and animal species, many of which we know little about. The loss of potential medicines is also great, as plant-derived ingredients figure in some 40 percent of prescription drugs. The pressures of politics and population growth make the protection of the tropical rain forests very difficult, even though their loss may be irrevocable. Half the world's original rain forests are already gone.

70

Isabela, Galápagos Islands

The Galápagos archipelago lies about 965 km (598 miles) off the coast of Ecuador in the Pacific Ocean. There are 19 islands in the archipelago, with a total land area of about 10,000 sq km (6,200 sq mi). The islands are formed of lava from shield volcanoes, which have broad, rounded cones. The volcanoes rise 2,100 to 3,000 m (7,000 to 10,000 feet) above the seafloor and up to another 1,700 m (5,600 feet) above sea level. At the base, many of the volcanoes are 16 to 32 km (10 to 20 miles) across. This image shows Isabela Island, which occupies more than half the total land area of the archipelago, and tiny Fernandina Island. The highest peak, Cerro Azul (1,689 m/5,540 feet), is found on Isabela (right). The Galápagos became famous after Charles Darwin visited them in 1835 and studied a number of species of wildlife unique to the islands, including the Galápagos tortoise and several finches. He further developed his ideas about natural selection based on his observations of the animals there, which originated from mainland species and evolved to adapt to their isolated island environment.

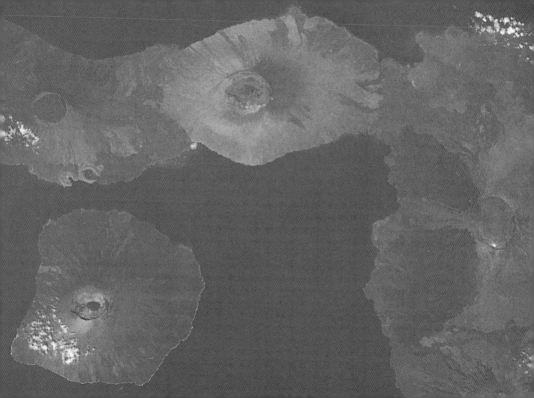

Bolivia: Altiplano

This image, obtained during the space shuttle *Discovery* mission of September 1991, is a view looking northeast over the *altiplano* (high plains) of Bolivia toward the Amazonian lowlands of Brazil. The two large white areas in the foreground are *salares,* or salt pans, which contain thick deposits of sodium chloride. The Salar de Coipasa is located to the left, and the Salar de Uyuni is located at the bottom of the image. During the recent geologic past, large lakes, similar to the large lake that once occupied the Great Salt Lake basin, occupied these basins, indicating that there have been major climatic changes in the region. Just to the north of the salares is Lago Poopó, a large saline lake only a few meters deep. The altiplano is bordered on the east and west by the Cordillera Oriental and Cordillera Occidental, respectively, divisions of the Andes with peaks topping 6,000 m (19,680 feet). The diagonal line across the top marks the Cordillera Oriental. Smoke from deforestation fires in the Amazon basin can be seen trapped at low altitude by the mountains. Lake Titicaca is farther north on the altiplano, but is not visible in this image.

74

Lake Titicaca

Lake Titicaca straddles the border between Peru and Bolivia in the Andes. The lake is located in the northern part of the Bolivian altiplano at 3,812 m (12,505 feet) above sea level, making it the highest major lake in the world. With a surface area of 8,300 sq km (3,200 sq mi), a length of 209 km (130 miles), and a maximum depth of 285 m (935 feet), it is the world's 20th-largest freshwater lake. The lake is separated into two basins by the Strait of Tiquina. A major pre-Incan population center called Tiahuanaco was located along the southern shores of Huiñaimarca, the smaller, more southerly of the two basins. The snow-covered Cordillera Real of the Andes is clearly visible along the eastern edge of the Lake Titicaca drainage basin. On the Peruvian side, there is an ancient volcano located between the main lake and Huiñaimarca. Several islands dot the lake, including the Islands of the Sun and the Moon, which were sacred to the Inca.

Atacama Desert, Chile

The Atacama Desert of northern Chile is one of the driest places on Earth (averaging less than 1 mm of rain per year in places) and suffers a complete lack of vegetation, as seen in this Landsat image. The extreme aridity in this region is caused in part by the dry air that descends in the subtropical high centered at about 30° S latitude. Upwelling of the cold Peruvian ocean current, which emanates from Antarctica, keeps the coastal area cooler than normal at these latitudes. Similar deserts caused by the same conditions are found along the western coasts of Africa and Australia. Sodium nitrate mines, which were active in the 19th century as a source for manufacturing explosive powder and fertilizer, show up as pale areas in the desert. The nitrate mining industry collapsed in the 20th century with the advent of synthetic nitrate. The low-grade copper ores of the region are now being mined. The Atacama Fault, the vertical linear feature near the center of the image, is one of many such features along South America's western coast. Antofagasta, a port located in a bay on the Pacific Ocean at the top left of the image, serves the area's mining interests.

78

Patagonia, Argentina

Patagonia is located in southern South America, including parts of Chile and Argentina. A barren, semiarid, inhospitable land, it is sparsely populated. This image shows Lagos Viedma (upper right) and Argentino (lower center), in Argentina. The Cordillera Darwin, part of the Andes range, covered in part by clouds and in part by snow in this image, extends diagonally from top right to bottom left. The border between Chile (left) and Argentina runs along this part of the cordillera. Today, several glaciers flow from the mountains into the lakes, producing potentially dangerous conditions when they advance very rapidly. The glaciers can also "calve" large blocks of ice into the lakes, just as tidewater glaciers release large volumes of ice into the ocean in southeastern Alaska. This region was covered by more extensive glaciers during the last major period of glaciation 10,000 years ago. Today the Patagonian ice fields of Hielo Norte and Hielo Sur (not shown here) contain a significant proportion of the modern glacial ice outside Antarctica and Greenland.

Europe

Europe covers 6,433,867 sq km (3,997,929 sq mi). It extends from North Cape, Norway, south to Cape Tarifa, Spain, and as far west as Iceland. Contiguous with Asia, it is separated from that continent by the Ural Mountains, the Ural River, the Caspian Sea, and the Black Sea. This composite image of Europe and northern Africa in summer highlights land cover type. Tundra, present mainly in the Russian Arctic, appears pink. Semiarid to arid regions, such as Africa and portions of the Iberian Peninsula, are yellow. Vegetative cover, present throughout most of Europe, is green. Despite the high latitudes of the British Isles (on a par with that of cold northern Canada), and Scandinavia (as far north as ice-covered southern Greenland), extensive vegetation blankets these areas because of the moderating influence of the warm North Atlantic current. Europe has three major seas—the Mediterranean, the Black, and the Baltic—all of which have restricted connections to other bodies of water. High evaporation and low rainfall make the Mediterranean Sea highly saline, while relatively high freshwater input to the Baltic and Black seas results in low salinity.

Europe: City Lights

Nighttime city lights circumscribe the European continent and demonstrate the uneven distribution of the population. Outlined clockwise from lower left are the Iberian Peninsula, France, the British Isles, Scandinavia, and the Russian Arctic coast. Between Britain and Norway, gas flares on offshore oil and gas drilling platforms light up the North Sea. The large pair of light clusters in northwestern Europe is formed by London and its environs in England, on the left, and the cities of northern France, Brussels and Antwerp in Belgium, Rotterdam and Amsterdam in the Netherlands, and cities of the Rhine and Ruhr valleys in Germany. The bright lights of Paris appear as a single large white dot beneath the two larger clusters. Much of central Europe is dark, while Moscow and St. Petersburg shine as two bright dots of light near the center of the image. The lights of Spain's eastern coast, the French Riviera, and the boot of Italy define the Mediterranean coast. At the southeastern end of the Mediterranean (bottom center) the Nile River valley and delta are clearly outlined.

British Isles

The British Isles sit on Europe's continental shelf, separated from the mainland (France) by the English Channel, which narrows at the Strait of Dover. The colors in this image approximate natural tones. The large island encompasses Scotland, in the north; Wales, in the southwest; and England, which includes the large peninsula in the far southwest. Ireland includes Northern Ireland, part of the United Kingdom, and the Republic of Ireland. Northwest of Scotland are the Outer Hebrides; to the northeast are the Orkney Islands. The small island in the Irish Sea, between Ireland and Britain, is the Isle of Man. Glacial erosion of the Scottish landscape produced the deeply eroded valleys, or glens, which are aligned with geologic faults in the basement rock. Lochs (lakes) are glens that have been filled in with either fresh or salt water. Loch Ness, home of the fabled monster, is located along the northern end of the prominent fault running from southwest to northeast in northern Scotland. The west coast of Ireland was formed by the geologic process of submergence: As river valleys sank, salt water filled them, creating oceanic bays.

London and Southeastern England

This Landsat image of southeastern England shows London, the whitish-green patch left of center, the Thames River and its estuary, and the Dover coast (far right). The green coloration represents vegetation: croplands in the top half, meadows and forests in the bottom half. Access via the Thames to the English Channel, the Atlantic Ocean, and the North Sea made London a natural port city. Water gates were employed to hold in water to keep ships afloat at low tide. However, the docks were closed in the early 1980s due to changes in the industry, and little shipping occurs there today. The funnel shape of the Thames estuary has often caused flooding in London, when easterly winds and storm tides drive seawater upriver in wavelike surges. To guard against floods, a series of embankments and downstream barriers was developed. The dark blue of the English Channel represents clear open water, and the even light blue is shallow water overlying sandbanks. Areas of streaky light blue indicate heavy water pollution.

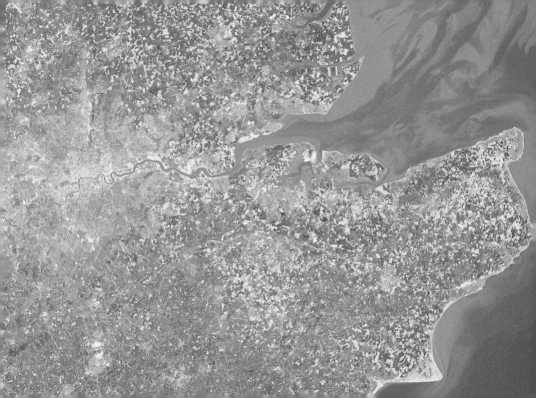

Iceland: Southeastern Coastline

Iceland, pictured here, lies 917 km (570 miles) west of Norway, just below the Arctic Circle. This large island (102,828 sq km/39,702 sq mi) has been built up by successive volcanic eruptions over the past 60 million years, with almost every type of volcano on Earth represented here. Most characteristic are the rows of craters formed by fissure eruptions typical of the Mid-Atlantic Ridge, on which the island sits. Iceland appears to lie over a hot spot in Earth's mantle, where a concentration of internal heat results in the upward movement of magma (molten rock), which rises to the surface and erupts as lava. Geothermal energy associated with volcanism is used by approximately 70 percent of the population of Iceland—some 250,000 people—to heat their homes. Although vast amounts of ice are visible in this photograph—including Europe's largest glacier, Vatnajökull (up to 900 m/3,000 feet thick, 8,409 sq km/3,247 sq mi)—ice fields and glaciers cover only about 10 percent of the country. Less than 1 percent of the land is arable because there has been little soil formation.

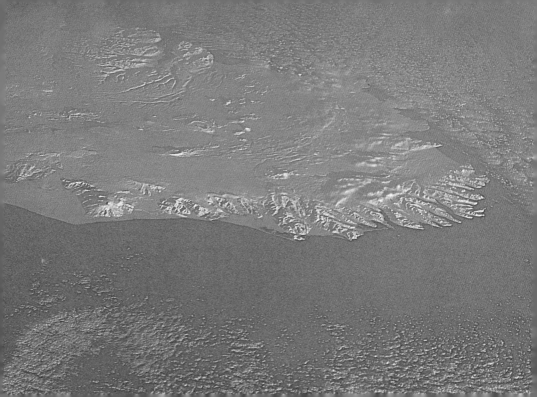

Norway: Oslo and Fjords

Oslo, the blue patch at the top center of this Landsat picture, is located at the head of 97-km (60-mile) long Oslo Fjord, an inlet of the Skagerrak, which is an arm of the North Sea. Founded in A.D. 1050, Oslo is the capital of Norway and the center of Norwegian trade, banking, fishing, and industry. The city is built on ancient beaches that were formed as a result of sea-level fluctuations during the Pleistocene ice ages. Surrounding the city are glacially rounded hills. During the last glacial advance, which reached its peak about 18,000 years ago, this entire region was covered by the Fennoscandian ice sheet. Glacial scouring and erosion have contoured the landscape. Most obvious are the numerous fjords—long, narrow, deep inlets that are the seaward ends of glacial valleys that have been filled with seawater. The approximately parallel orientation of the fjords and lakes seen here results from the uniform direction of glacial advance and retreat.

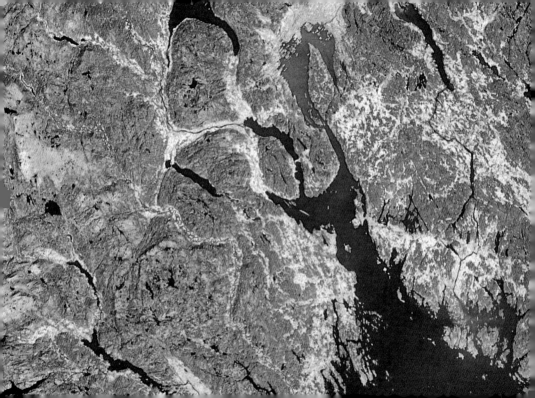

Ems Estuary, Netherlands

The Ems estuary, which forms part of the international border between Germany (center right) and the Netherlands, is pictured in this Landsat image. The river flows from the right into the square-shaped basin known as the Dollart before emptying into the North Sea. The Frisian Islands, off the coast, and the brown intertidal flats were formed by the extensive outflow of sediments through the Ems estuary. The Ems River drains almost 15,000 sq km (6,000 sq mi) of northwestern Europe. Much of the land pictured here is below sea level, protected from marine incursion by man-made seawalls and drainage systems. The small coastal inlet on the left is the Lauwers Zee. The brownish area in the lower center is the city of Groningen, Netherlands. The rectangular pattern that dominates much of the photograph represents extensive cultivation of the terrain.

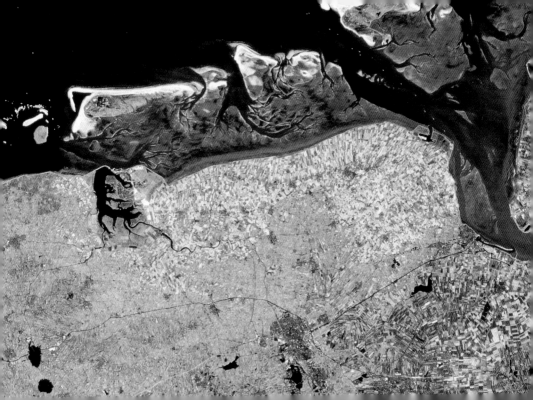

Netherlands: Land Reclamation

Because nearly one-fourth of the Netherlands is below sea level, land reclamation is an important national project. This Landsat image shows land reclamation in the IJsselmeer, which was once a shallow inlet of the North Sea known as the Zuider Zee. A dam, the Afluntsdijk, the faint diagonal line spanning the waterway in the left center of the picture, was built between 1927 and 1932. This dam now separates the saline Wadden Zee to the north from the southern IJsselmeer, a freshwater lake. Large areas along the IJsselmeer were then dammed off and drained, creating fertile land that is excellent for agriculture. Examples of this land, once submerged underwater and now used for farming, appear just below center: Noordoostpolder (top) and Flevoland (bottom). Also visible in this photograph are the barrier islands, the Frisians, to the north of the continent, which protect the coastline of the Netherlands from the North Sea. White, sandy beaches line the seaward side of these islands. The Ems estuary is in the top right corner.

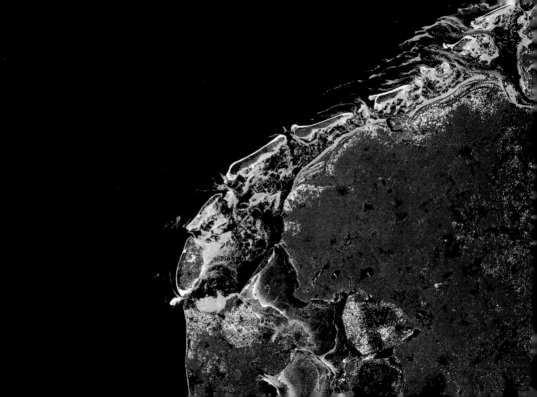

Zeeland, Netherlands

Zeeland, pictured in this Landsat image, is the island complex formed by the estuaries of the Rhine and Schelde rivers. The shape of Zeeland's coastline is constantly changing as islands are enlarged by alluvial deposition, united and protected by dikes, or washed away by floods. Major flooding on February 1, 1953, resulted in more than 1,800 deaths and prompted implementation of the Delta Project to dam major sea channels and further connect islands with one another. Along the northern bank of the Rhine, which runs east to west in the top of the photograph, is the city of Rotterdam. Only 30 km (19 miles) from the North Sea, Rotterdam developed as a fishing village and early on became a major port for the region. Today's economy is almost totally based on shipping, as the Rhine connects the city with western and central Europe. In the lower center of the photograph, a thin curving line represents part of a long canal system that links Rotterdam to Antwerp, Belgium, which lies on the Schelde River to the south of the area shown in the photograph.

98

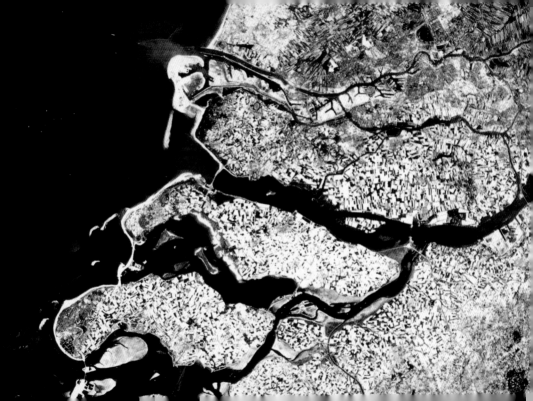

Hamburg, Germany

Hamburg, Germany, built on the banks of the Elbe River where it is joined by the Alster and Bille rivers, is pictured in this Landsat image. The Elbe splits just upstream of the city; its branches rejoin on the city's western side. Excellent access to the North Sea, 109 km (68 miles) downstream via the river, has made Hamburg a busy port city and an economic center for Germany. This deep estuary has been dredged since the late 19th century and can accommodate large ocean liners and freighters. The extensive systems of docks and canals lining the riverbanks were built for the voluminous ship traffic serviced by the city. The canals are characterized by their dark rectangular appearance. The inner city appears light brown, while the outer suburbs are greener in color. To the east and south of the city, a patchwork of farm fields is visible as rectangular strips of alternating colors.

Paris, France

Paris and its surroundings can be seen in this Satellite
Positioning and Tracking (SPOT) image. The capital of
France, Paris lies along the banks of the Seine River,
which meanders through this image on its way northwest
to the Bay of the Seine and the English Channel. Many of
the famous landmarks of Paris can be identified in this
photograph. On the north bank of the Seine is the Louvre
(upper center). On the south bank, just to the west, are
the Eiffel Tower and Ecole Militaire. Ile de la Cité, home
of Notre-Dame Cathedral, and Ile St-Louis are just to
the east of these famous landmarks. The red coloration,
representing vegetation, shows the locations of the many
famous gardens and woods in and around the city. The
Tuileries, at the head of the Louvre, and the Champs de
Mars, by the Eiffel Tower, are obvious, as is the large
Bois de Boulogne, southwest of the Arc de Triomphe.
The runways of Orly Airport are visible at the bottom
right. The palace of Versailles, with its decorative pools
(including the cross-shaped Grand Canal and the Pièce
d'Eau des Suisses), built by Louis XIV, is at lower left.

102

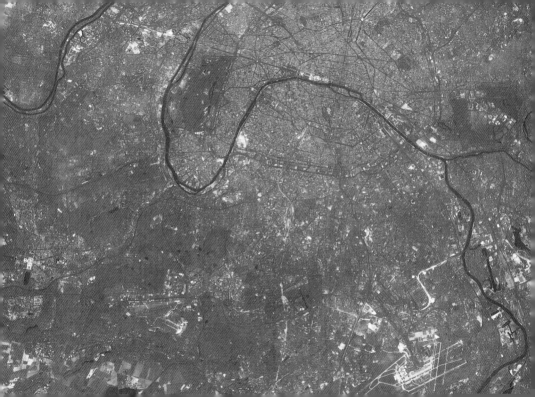

Strait of Gibraltar

The Strait of Gibraltar is the narrow passageway connecting the open Atlantic Ocean (west) to the closed basin of the Mediterranean Sea (east). In ancient times, the 23-km (14-mile) stretch between the Pillars of Hercules—the Rock of Gibraltar in Europe and Jebel Musa in Ceuta, Africa—demarcated the western end of the civilized world. At its narrowest point, the strait is only 14 km (9 miles) wide, restricting water flow between the two bodies. A submerged series of sills appears as underwater cliffs. In the photograph, Spain lies to the north, with Punta Marroqui and its lighthouse (seen as a white dot) extending farthest south into the Mediterranean. Gibraltar, to the east of the stretch of Spanish coastline pictured here, is a British colony. Morocco, Africa, is the landmass to the south, though the small peninsula to the east, Ceuta, is governed by Spain. The city of Tangier, Morocco, can be seen as the white patch in the embayment in the lower left.

104

Italian Alps and Lombardy Plain

The Alps represent a convergent tectonic boundary, formed by the collision of two enormous continental landmasses. Beginning 40 million years ago, the collision has uplifted and folded continental crust at the line of contact, the Alps. Most of the range consists of sedimentary rock layers that have been folded under intense pressure. The current landscape shows modification through glacial action, with higher elevations remaining covered by snow and ice. The eastern Italian Alps, known as the Dolomites, the Lombardy plain, and the city of Venice are visible in this Landsat image. Venice's lagoon and the Grand Canal (the squiggle crossing the lower half of the city) can be seen in the lower right. As sediment is eroded from the Alps, it travels downstream, extending the Lombardy plain into the Adriatic Sea. The whitish streaks over the plain illustrate this process. The alluvial plain continues to grow, providing agricultural land rich in nutrients. The dark patch in the lower left is Lake Garda. The city of Verona is the blue-gray patch to its right.

Rome, Italy

Located in central Italy on the Tiber River, Rome and the autonomous Vatican City are situated only 24 km (15 miles) from the Tyrrhenian Sea, a division of the Mediterranean, seen in the lower left corner of this image. The densely populated city is visible as a bluish-green region straddling the upper Tiber. Rome was built on the famous seven hills, all of volcanic origin, on a marshland that was once considered a malarial plain (a breeding ground for malaria-carrying mosquitoes). The prominent topographic feature to the southeast, approximately 25 km (16 miles) from Rome, is Monte Cavo, an extinct volcano whose highlands are known as the Colli Albani (the Alban Hills). The hills are dotted with towns known collectively as Castelli Romani (Roman castles), which were once the villas and castles of wealthy and prominent Romans. The most famous is Castel Gandolfo, the pope's summer residence, located on Lago di Albano, the larger lake in the volcano's crater. The small, round Lago di Nemi is also known as the "Mirror of Diana," the ancient Roman goddess.

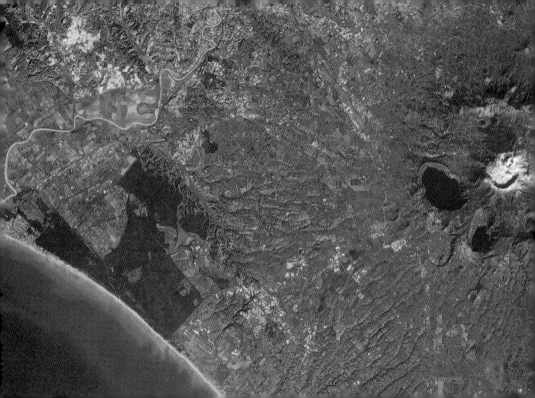

Mount Etna, Sicily

Mount Etna, on the island of Sicily, is the highest active volcano in Europe, at approximately 3,323 m (10,902 feet) high. Geologic characteristics indicate that the volcano has been active for some 2.5 million years. History has recorded more than 260 eruptions since 1500 B.C., some of which have been extremely violent. One of the deadliest, in 1669, was accompanied by an earthquake that resulted in more than 20,000 fatalities. Etna erupted for several months in 1992. Although eruptions can be deadly and destructive, the volcanic soil on the lower slopes is nutrient-rich and excellent for agricultural use. For this reason, the base is densely populated. In this Landsat image, two patches of white can be seen at Etna's summit. The white patch on the western side is snow cover at the peak, which remains most of the year. To the east, a plume of smoke and steam is visible. Sicilian coastal cities are indicated by the blue patches along the Ionian coast. The Ionian Sea is the part of the Mediterranean directly beneath the boot of Italy.

110

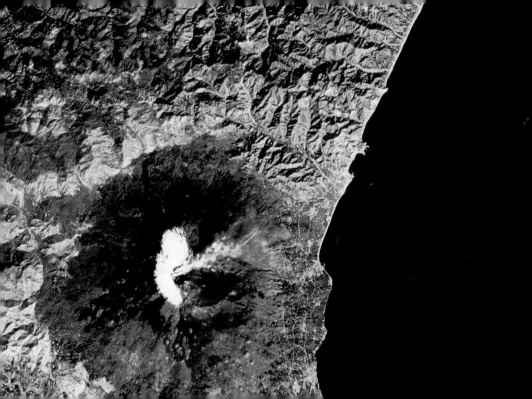

Africa

Africa is the second-largest of the continents, with an area of 30,149,600 sq km (11,596,000 sq mi), and is the only continent centered on the equator. It contains vast deserts, deep rain forests, long, meandering rivers, and thousands of miles of coastline on the Atlantic and Indian oceans and the Mediterranean and Red seas. Depicted in tan and brown in this image, the Sahara stretches across northern Africa, with the semiarid grasslands of the Sahel beneath it. The red and green vegetated regions of the tropical rain forest, centered on the Congo River, contrast sharply with the dry regions. Lake Victoria, which feeds into the Nile, and the long, linear lakes of the Great Rift Valley appear as black shapes in southeastern Africa. The island of Madagascar lies in the Indian Ocean off the southeastern coast. Africa lacks the long, linear mountain chains that characterize all other continents and has relatively few earthquakes. In the upper right-hand corner of this photograph is the Arabian Peninsula, separated from Africa by the Red Sea.

Sinai Peninsula

Noted for its strategic location and valuable deposits of manganese and petroleum, the Sinai Peninsula sits at the mouth of the Red Sea between the Gulf of Suez, to the west, and the Gulf of 'Aqaba, to the east. The Suez Canal lies at the northern end of the Gulf of Suez. Directly north of the Gulf of 'Aqaba is the Dead Sea, which contains no life and lies 392 m (1,286 feet) below sea level. Egypt, including the Nile River and its delta, lies to the west, and Jordan and Saudi Arabia are to the east, with Israel occupying the northeastern corner of the peninsula. The border between Egypt and Israel forms a distinct line, reflecting the different rural landscapes of the two countries. The Mediterranean extends northward, covered by a haze that probably results from windblown dust rising from this arid region. Two major geologic units comprise the Sinai. A sparsely vegetated limestone plateau that slopes downward toward the Mediterranean is shaded yellow. To the south, darker colors depict a mountainous region composed of igneous rocks that are sharply incised by deep, canyonlike wadis, or dry streambeds.

Suez Canal

The Suez Canal, built by the French and opened to navigation on November 17, 1869, runs along the Sinai Peninsula, connecting the Red Sea to the Mediterranean. The canal is 160 km (100 miles) long, has a minimum width of 55 m (180 feet), and can accommodate ships with drafts as deep as 20 m (66 feet). Its construction greatly reduced shipping time between Europe and southern and eastern Asia. The excavation of the canal was rapid and easy, thanks to soft soils and the use of existing lakes, such as Great Bitter Lake (bottom center) and Lake Timsah (the small lake above Great Bitter Lake). Port Said, Egypt, sits at the canal's entryway on a strip of sand in the Mediterranean. The red coloration in the left of the photograph represents vegetation along the low-lying Nile Delta, while the thinner red line to the south borders the freshwater Ismailia Canal, which supplies the area with drinking water. The dark blue area in the upper left, seaward of the delta, is Lake Manzala. A long chain of sandy barrier islands in the upper right protects Sabkhet el Bardawil, on the Sinai Peninsula, from the Mediterranean.

116

Nile Delta and Cairo

The world's longest river, the Nile covers a distance of 6,671 km (4,145 miles). It starts in Burundi, passes through Lake Victoria, and continues northward to the Mediterranean, where it has built up an enormous low-lying, fan-shaped delta. This color-enhanced Landsat image of the Nile Delta illustrates changes in land use in the area between 1972/73 and 1989/90. The large red area depicts land that has been used for agricultural purposes since at least 1972/73. The blue regions are new agricultural lands that have been reclaimed from the desert through irrigation. Blue-green regions near the coast are lagoons and wetlands that have been partially reclaimed. The magenta areas show urban encroachment upon the desert. Cairo, the capital of Egypt, appears as a greenish patch with a partial ring of yellow, marking urban development on previously agricultural land. The Nile was dammed in 1970 at Aswân, in southern Egypt, in order to improve irrigation and provide hydroelectric power. However, many environmental problems have resulted, such as the loss of fertile silt behind the dam and the salinization of soils.

118

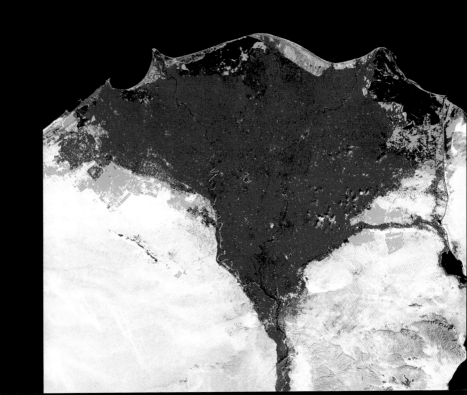

Sudan: Sahara

About one-fifth of Earth's human population inhabits deserts, which cover one-third of the planet's land area. This view of the Sahara in Sudan, Africa's largest country, was taken from the space shuttle *Atlantis* in 1992. The Sahara is the largest subtropical desert in the world, covering almost all of northern Africa. Its 9,065,000 sq km (3,500,000 sq mi) span lands both low and high, from 30 m (100 feet) below sea level to 3,400 m (11,000 feet) above. It has rich deposits of many metals and vast underground reserves of oil and natural gas. Daytime temperatures have reached 55°C (130°F). In this photograph, old lava flows are visible as the dark areas at the top and bottom left. These lava flows were extruded over an ancient soil that shows up as outcrops of brownish tableland. This is surrounded by a reddish midlayer, seen over most of the photograph. The light bottom layer is exposed in the valleys. These Saharan soils most likely formed in an ancient forest or savanna, which disappeared as the climate became drier and more hostile to vegetation.

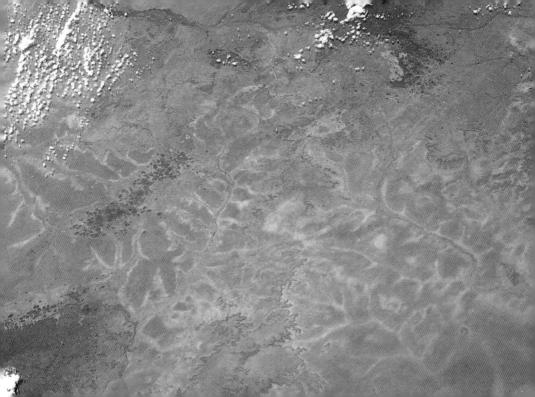

Anti-Atlas Mountains, Morocco

This Landsat image shows the Anti-Atlas Mountains, which, with the High and Middle Atlas ridges, comprise the Atlas Mountains. This group forms a natural barrier between the fertile coastal plain of northwestern Morocco and the Sahara. Morocco, in northern Africa, lies across the Strait of Gibraltar from Spain. These mountains were formed by ancient collisional motion between the African and Eurasian tectonic plates. The boundary of the plates is fairly stable today. The banded appearance of the mountain range was caused by uplift and folding of the rocks, which was followed by weathering and erosion. The green linear feature running through the center of the photograph is the Oued Draa River valley, a generally dry watercourse that fills only during periods of rain. The rugged terrain, aridity, and sparse vegetation of this region make it inhospitable and have helped to maintain the relative isolation of its inhabitants, Berber tribespeople.

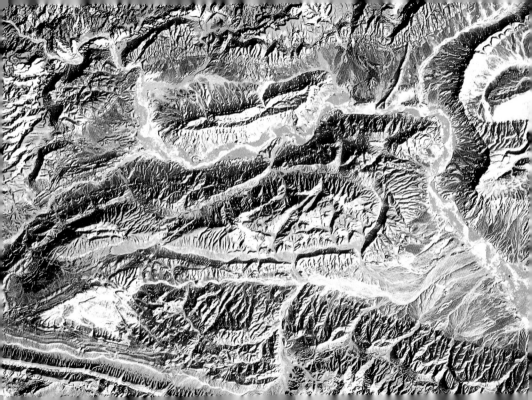

Richat Structure, Sahara

For many years, scientists believed the 40-km (25-mile) diameter Richat Structure of Mauritania, in northwestern Africa, to be an impact crater caused by a meteorite. Recent geologic work, however, indicates that it is an uplifted dome of rocks. Erosion of the roof of the dome has exposed this cross-sectional view, in which the inward-tilting rock layers can be observed. In this April 1991 space shuttle photograph, the different rock units appear as the rings in a bull's-eye pattern. In geologic structures of this type, the oldest rocks are located in the center, with successively younger rocks toward the exterior. The Richat Structure is located on the edge of the Adrar Plateau in the northern part of Mauritania, which sits on Africa's northwestern Atlantic coast, between Western Sahara and Senegal.

Lake Chad

Lake Chad, the fourth-largest lake in Africa, is the dark gray area in the center of this space shuttle photograph. The lake is located in the Sahel, a semiarid grassland zone south of the Sahara that is peopled by nomadic shepherds. It is in central Africa, at the conjunction of the countries of Chad, Cameroon, Nigeria, and Niger. Lake Chad's volume fluctuates seasonally with changes in the ratio of precipitation to evaporation, and its surface area can double in size from the dry season to the wet season. Chad's water levels serve as an index of drought throughout north-central Africa. Lake Chad has been photographed from space many times over the past 20 years, so we have excellent documentation of the decrease in its size, which continues today. The reduction is indicated by the sand dunes just north of the lake, which were previously submerged. The clouds that can be seen at the bottom of the photograph are not rain-producing clouds.

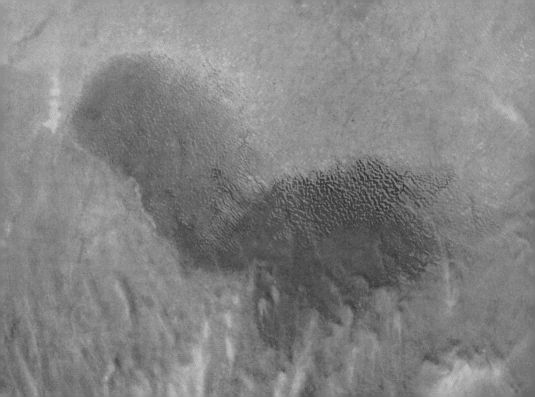

Lake Natron, Tanzania

Lake Natron is a soda, or sodium carbonate, lake in East Africa's Great Rift Valley in Tanzania. The Great Rift, which extends from Jordan in southwestern Asia to Mozambique in southeastern Africa, was formed by two crustal plates pulling apart. At low-lying areas the rift has been filled in with water; the Dead and Red seas are two such bodies. The red color of Lake Natron is caused by blooms of various algae and the chemistry of the water, which has a high concentration of sodium carbonate. The whitish spots seen in part of the lake are drying beds of sodium carbonate, which comes from the nearby carbonatite volcanoes, one at the northern end and one at the bottom right. The southern part of the lake has a different flow pattern from the rest, so it is clear of algae. Because of the lake's unusual chemistry, few types of fish can live in its waters. However, the lake is home to hundreds of thousands of pink flamingos, who feed on the abundant algae. Lake Natron is the only known East African breeding ground for these birds.

128

Ngorongoro Crater, Tanzania

Ngorongoro Crater (lower center), the largest intact
caldera in the world (17 km/11 miles in diameter), and
surrounding volcanoes in northern Tanzania are
highlighted in this Landsat picture. The volcano from
which Ngorongoro Crater resulted was formed during
the fracturing that created the Great Rift Valley of Africa
15 to 20 million years ago. Ngorongoro reached its peak
height 2 to 3 million years ago, when it was as tall as
Mount Kilimanjaro, the highest mountain in Africa.
Inward collapse lowered the mountain, and today the
crater rim rises 2,400 m (7,873 feet) above sea level;
the crater's floor lies 1,700 m (5,576 feet) below the rim.
The caldera is the site of Tanzania's Ngorongoro
National Park, established in 1956 as one of Africa's
major conservation areas, with plentiful wildlife and the
densest predator population in Africa. To the northwest
of Ngorongoro lie Olduvai Gorge, where the Leakey
family of paleontologists found many early hominid
remains, and the Serengeti Plain. Lakes Eyasi (left)
and Manyara appear at the bottom of this image.

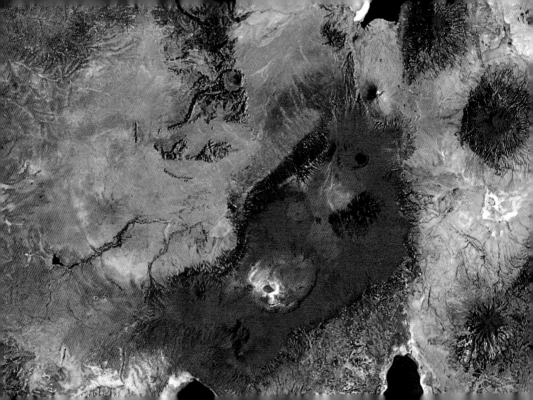

Mount Kilimanjaro

Mount Kilimanjaro is a huge volcanic complex straddling the border between Kenya to the north and Tanzania to the south. The complex measures approximately 80 km (50 miles) from east to west, and consists of three eruptive centers: Kibo, Mawenzi, and Shira. Kibo, the highest of these, is the highest peak in Africa, with an elevation of 5,895 m (19,340 feet). Geologically speaking, Kilimanjaro is a new mountain; its vents have been spewing lava for only the past million years. The most recent volcanic activity was in the 1930s. Because of its great height, Kilimanjaro is snow-capped despite its equatorial position and is one of the few sites within the tropics where glaciers can be found. In this Landsat image, the various vegetation belts around the mountain can be seen as concentric circles. Moving from outside in, these zones are the pale outlying savanna, lighter green zones where coffee and bananas are cultivated, darker green montane forest, a black heather zone, and an alpine zone. The vegetation ends completely as the summit is approached.

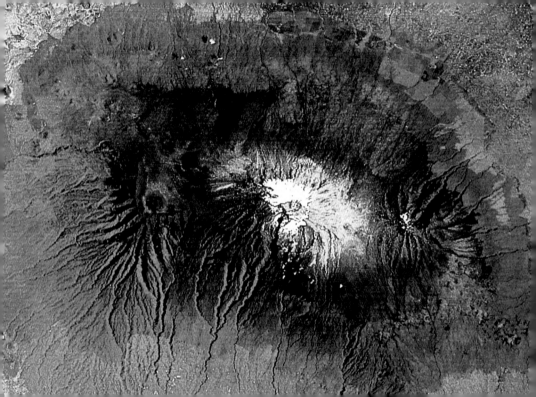

Namib Sand Sea, Namibia

This view of the Namib Sand Sea, part of the Namib Desert, which extends for 2,000 km (1,240 miles) along the southwestern coast of Africa, was taken by the space shuttle *Atlantis* in 1991. The Namibian highlands can be seen at the right of the photograph. Rainwater that drains from the highlands flows west through the area at the center of the image to form a river partly bisecting the sand sea. Today, the volume of water is small, and the river dries up in the area at the left edge of the photograph, where whitish deposits of salt are visible. During wetter times 15 to 18 million years ago, however, the river was powerful enough to carve a gorge up to 30 m (98 feet) deep. Southwesterly winds have created the semilinear pattern of most of the sand dunes, which reach lengths up to 50 km (31 miles) and stand 60 to 100 m (197 to 328 feet) high. The star-shaped dunes on both sides of the river, which range up to 325 m (1,066 feet) tall, are formed by winds blowing from east to west along the river valley.

Brandberg Mountain, Namib Desert

This view of Brandberg Mountain in the western Namib Desert, taken during a 1993 space shuttle mission, clearly highlights the circular structure of the volcano. The Brandberg massif consists of a granite core formed during volcanic activity about 180 million years ago and gradually exposed through erosion; at its highest it reaches 2,630 m (8,626 feet). The mountain is noted for the several hundred Stone Age rock paintings at sites on its sides. Heavy clouds and fog are visible in the bottom left of the photograph; the cloud banks extend only a few miles inland, however. Although scattered clouds can be seen to the north and east, most of the moisture in this extremely arid region comes from coastal fog. Some dry river valleys can also be spotted in the photograph. Flash flooding fills the rivers during the rainy season, but they remain dry the rest of the year.

Great Dyke, Zimbabwe

The Great Dyke, in the south-central African nation of Zimbabwe, is a set of four igneous formations that through a process measuring radioactive decay have been dated as approximately 2.55 billion years old. The dike complex is 480 km (298 miles) long and averages 10 km (6 miles) in width. Dikes are geologic structures, also known as intrusions, that occur when molten rock, or magma, emerges through fissures in Earth's crust. This magma then spreads out laterally along planes of weakness in Earth's crust like sandwich filling between two pieces of bread. The Great Dyke is composed of ultrabasic and basic rocks, which have high concentrations of magnesium and iron and no or almost no silica. Rock types found here include chromite, pyroxenite, peridotite, and gabbro, and minerals include ores containing gold, silver, chromium, platinum, and nickel. Mica and asbestos are also mined. This photograph was taken by the space shuttle *Endeavour* during a January 1993 mission.

Madagascar

Madagascar, the world's fourth-largest island, lies 400 km (248 miles) off the southeastern coast of Africa, across from Mozambique. Today, the island nation faces severe environmental problems, the results of slash-and-burn agriculture, overgrazing, and excessive logging in a land whose steep topography and torrential rains exacerbate soil erosion. The southeast trade winds carry moisture from the Indian Ocean, resulting in annual rainfall of nearly 4,000 mm (156 inches) in some parts of the island. On Madagascar's central plateau, the intense chemical weathering that occurs when rainwater interacts with rock produces a soil rich in iron oxide and aluminum hydroxide. Nowadays, these clays are being rapidly washed to sea as the vegetation that once anchored the soil is lost. Tan sediment plumes of these minerals can be seen along the coast. Scientists estimate that from 75 to 90 percent of the country's original rain forest has already been destroyed. Loss of habitat has led to the endangerment of many native species, including varieties of lemurs unique to the island.

Asia

Asia, covering 44,391,163 sq km (17,139,445 sq mi), is the largest continent. Eurasia, the combination of the European and Asian continents (pictured here), is the world's largest landmass, with an area of 54,106,000 sq km (20,890,300 sq mi). Encompassing almost half of the land surface of Earth, it extends from Ireland (upper left) to the Chukotski Peninsula of Russia (top right), which was once connected to Alaska by the Bering Land Bridge. The two continents have no clear dividing line, although it has traditionally been placed at the Ural and Caucasus mountains. Within its boundaries Asia embraces every climate and land type (polar, tropical, alpine, desert), claiming the highest (Mount Everest, 8,848 m/29,028 feet) and lowest (Dead Sea, 392 m/1,286 feet below sea level) elevations on Earth. The colors in this mosaic image represent different types of land surface cover. Red shows vegetation, and gray is semidesert. The sands of Arabia are white. The red and white mottling in Southeast Asia (to the right of India) is tropical forest. Russia is the largest country on the continent, with an area of more than 17,000,000 sq km (6,500,000 sq mi).

142

Laristan, Iran

Iran, known as Persia until 1935, lies on a high plateau rimmed by mountain ranges, with salt deserts in the interior. The subsurface geologic environment yields large quantities of oil but is also prone to earthquakes, some of which have been severe. This Landsat image of southern Iran clearly shows sedimentary strata that were folded during the collision of the Iranian and Arabian tectonic plates. Both soft and resistant rock types make up the folded strata; differential erosion, which accentuates the various types, has produced the valleys and ridges. This region, near the Persian Gulf coast, is part of the Makran ranges, which cover an area 240 km by 480 km (149 by 298 miles). In this part of the country, elevations are generally less than 1,500 m (4,900 feet) above sea level, although some peaks surpass 2,100 m (7,000 feet). The landscape is hot and dry with few perennial streams, and groundwater supplies tend to be very brackish.

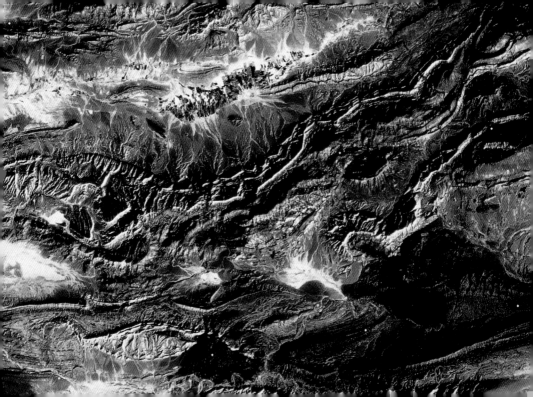

Aral Sea

The Aral Sea is a large saline lake on the border between Kazakhstan and Uzbekistan, former republics of the USSR just east of the Caspian Sea. The Aral is disappearing rapidly because a large amount of water is being removed from the Syr Darya and Amu Darya, two rivers entering the lake from the southwest, for the irrigation of cotton and rice fields. The Aral Sea is in a closed basin with no outlet. Evaporation has increased the salinity, decimating the fish population and destroying the fishing industry. Large salt flats have been exposed, from which salt is transported into the atmosphere by the wind. The region is very arid, as it receives only about 100 mm (3.94 inches) of precipitation annually. The Aral Sea has shrunk by 40 percent since 1960 and could disappear completely by the 21st century, unless the irrigation of the rice and cotton crops is curtailed.

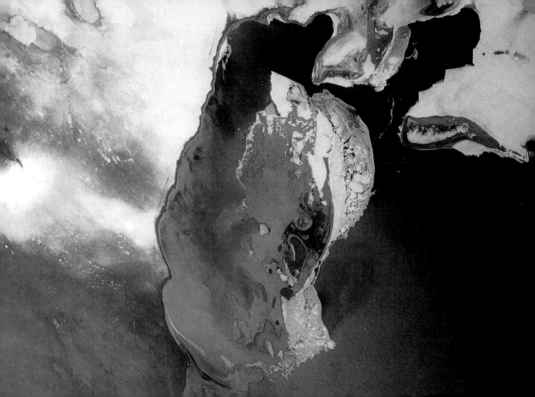

Turfan Depression, China

The Turfan (or Turpan) Depression, in the lower part of this image, is located in northwestern China just to the southeast of the town of Urümqi, the capital of the Xinjiang Uygur region. Created by faulting, the basin is 50,000 sq km (19,500 sq mi) in area and descends to 154 m (505 feet) below sea level at Aydingkol Hu (lake). Mean annual rainfall in the basin is generally less than 30 mm (1.17 inches). The basin is intensively farmed (the red areas indicate vegetation), and although it is irrigable, drought and blowing sand are major problems. Average temperatures in the basin vary between −10°C (14°F) in January and 32°C (90°F) in July. However, daily temperature variations can be extreme, and the thermometer can reach 54°C (129°F) in summer. The large brown area to the right of the basin is a sand desert. North of the basin towers the eastern extremity of the Tien Shan (Celestial Mountains), whose peaks top 6,000 m (19,680 feet) in elevation. Lower mountains border the basin on the south. Today there are glaciers along the crest of the Tien Shan, and there is evidence that more extensive glaciation occurred in the past.

Himalayas, Nepal

The Himalayas occupy the top half of this Landsat image. Mount Everest (8,848 m/29,021 feet), the highest mountain in the world, casts a shadow at the head of the valley in the top right portion of the image. It sits on the Nepal-Tibet border. The Himalayas, known as fold mountains, formed when the Indian and Asian tectonic plates collided. This collision was of such force that it caused the crust at the point of collision to buckle or fold up, forming the highest mountains on Earth today. The two plates continue to push against each other, and the mountains are still rising in elevation. The plain at the bottom of the image is in northern India, and the many rivers in this region are tributaries of the Ganges River. The Churia Ghati Hills are the darkest red color just north of the plain in the bottom half. With their celestial heights, the Himalayas have long attracted the adventurous and the spiritual. Mount Everest was first scaled successfully by Sir Edmund Hillary of New Zealand and Tenzing Norkay of Nepal on May 29, 1953.

Bangladesh: Ganges Delta

The People's Republic of Bangladesh lies west of the highlands of Myanmar (formerly Burma), east of India, and south of the foothills of the Himalayas. The Ganges River enters Bangladesh from the west and is joined by the Brahmaputra River from the north, just left of top center in this image, which approximates natural color. Farther south, the Meghna River joins the Ganges from the east near the capital city of Dacca (top center). The Ganges continues south into the Bay of Bengal through numerous channels that cross the Ganges Delta. Bangladesh has a population of about 100 million people in an area that is slightly smaller than the state of Wisconsin; the population density of the country is more than 700 people per sq km. Because of the low relief of the terrain and its high population density, it is susceptible to severely harmful natural disasters. The seasonal torrential rains often bring devastating floods to this low-lying area. A cyclone of April 1991 killed more than 130,000 people.

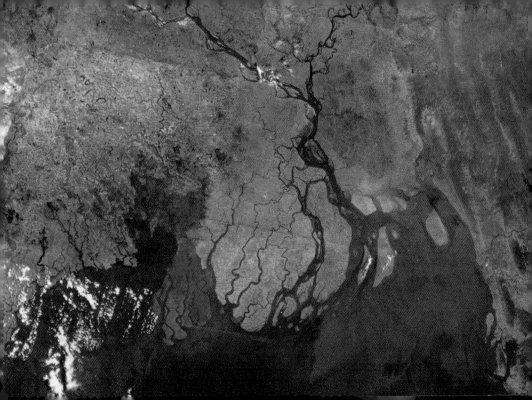

Indian Ocean: Maldive Islands

India and Sri Lanka are seen at an oblique angle in the top left portion of this image. The island of Sri Lanka, covered by a cloud that almost exactly follows its outline, is separated from India by the 64-km (40-mile) wide Palk Strait, which appears as a lighter shade of blue than the surrounding waters. The white ring structures that are visible in the bottom of the image are members of the Maldive chain of some 2,000 atolls, which are clusters of coral reefs enclosing lagoons. The formation of atolls is a long process that begins when an undersea volcano breaks the surface. Over time, corals build up the reef around the volcano's perimeter. Eventually, due in part to erosion and its own weight, the volcano subsides beneath the surface, leaving only the coral reef ring, which over time becomes an inhabitable landmass. The subsidence associated with these atolls is occurring because of movements of the Maldive oceanic ridge. The Maldives support a population of nearly 150,000 on a total land area of about 300 sq km (117 sq mi), all of which is nearly at sea level. Fishing is the chief industry.

Kamchatka Peninsula, Siberia

The Kamchatka Peninsula, located in the northeastern part of Siberia, separates the Sea of Okhotsk from the Bering Sea. Two parallel mountain ranges, separated by the Kamchatka River, run along the length of the 1,200-km (750-mile) long peninsula. Part of the Ring of Fire—a belt of volcanoes encircling the Pacific—the Kamchatka Peninsula has 127 volcanoes and suffers frequent and violent earthquakes. This photograph, obtained from the space shuttle *Discovery* in 1991, shows several volcanic cones. The higher ones are Sopka Gorely Khrebet (1,829 m/6,000 feet), at bottom left, and the larger Mutnovskaya Sopka (2,323 m/7,619 feet), to the right, along the bottom edge of the image. These volcanoes are on the southeastern coast of the peninsula, on the Bering Sea. One of the world's highest volcanoes, Klyuchevskaya Sopka (4,748 m/15,580 feet in elevation) is located north of this area near the center of the peninsula.

Yangtze Delta, China

The Yangtze River, or Chiang Jiang, is the fourth-longest river in the world (5,525 km/3,430 miles long). The river originates in the Kunlun Mountains of the Tibetan Plateau and crosses twelve Chinese provinces en route to the East China Sea. The Yangtze Delta begins beyond the city of Zhenjiang (Chen-chiang), in Jiangsu province. The river is only about 3 km (2 miles) wide near the head of the delta, but spreads into an 81-km (50-mile) wide estuary when it reaches the sea. There are a number of branches of the river on the delta and numerous lakes, the most notable being T'ai Hu. The river divides near its mouth to form two channels around the island Chongming Dao, which is visible in this Landsat image. The 780-sq-km (300-sq-mi) island apparently formed more than 1,000 years ago when alluvium blocked the channel of the river. Shanghai is the dark gray patch south of the island on the delta. Rice and cotton are major agricultural products of this low-lying region.

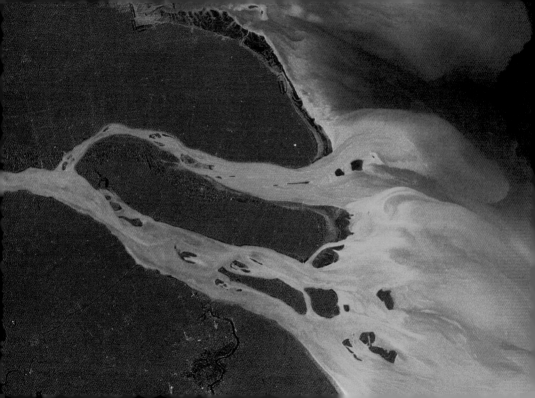

Tokyo, Japan

Japan consists of a series of islands dotted with volcanoes that were formed by the collision and subduction of two oceanic tectonic plates. Because one plate remains subducted beneath the other, the islands are subject to many earthquakes. In this Landsat image of the Tokyo metropolitan area, the blue indicates buildings and the red shows vegetation. Three main rivers, which have been channelized, run through the metropolitan area. The Arakawa-hosuiro (left) and the Edo-gawa (right) are the two rivers in the upper right. At the bottom left is the Tama-gawa. The runways of the Tokyo International Airport can be seen at its mouth. The capital of Japan, Tokyo is located on the east coast of the island of Honshu, which is the largest Japanese island. Tokyo Bay is a major natural port on the Pacific Ocean; the wharves that line the bay can be seen in this photograph. Many of the block-shaped islands in the port area are reclaimed land. Tokyo is very built up, with little parkland. The grounds and gardens of the Imperial Place, which appear red, stand out in the center of the image.

Sakurajima, Japan

Sakurajima is an active volcano located in Kagoshima Bay on the southern end of the Japanese island of Kyushu, which is the southernmost of the main islands. The volcano has erupted thousands of times since the eighth century, extremely violently in 1476 and 1779. One of its eruptions built up the land bridge that connects it to the mainland. Today the volcano continues to erupt, but the associated minor ash falls do not create major disturbances. A plume blows across the bay in this image. About half the landscape of the island of Kyushu is covered with rough volcanic landforms, which make agriculture difficult in these areas. The slopes of Sakurajima are extremely fertile because of its volcanic soil. There are some 200 other volcanoes throughout Japan, about a third of which have been active in historic times. The highest peak in Japan, Mount Fuji, is a volcano that rises to about 3,776 m (12,388 feet) above sea level. The islands of Japan are also susceptible to earthquakes because of tectonic movements. Approximately 1,500 earthquakes are registered yearly, most of which are not felt at the surface.

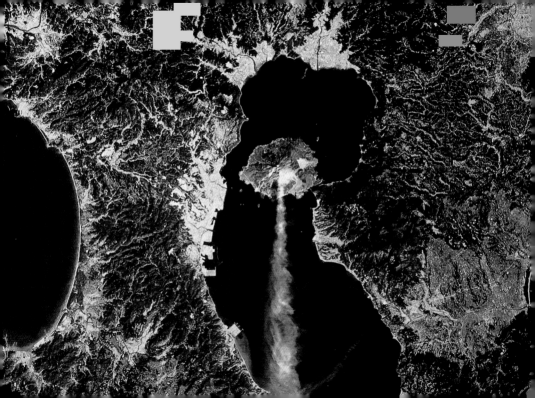

Mount Pinatubo, Philippines

The Philippines are an archipelago of 7,100 volcanic islands some 800 km (500 miles) off the southeast coast of Asia. Manila, the capital, is on the main island, Luzon. The volcanic Mount Pinatubo, also on Luzon, is located in the center of this image, taken from the space shuttle *Atlantis.* Recent volcanic activity, especially the series of eruptions in 1991, has produced extensive mud and ash deposits around the mountain. These deposits, which continue to wash down in rivers and streams, can be seen emanating from the center of the image. After a large eruption in June 1991, Clark Field, a major U.S. Air Force base, located to the east (right) of the mountain, was abandoned. Ash and other debris from such eruptions have spread around the globe through the atmosphere. This debris can lower global temperatures and cause more colorful sunsets for years. Volcanic events can be detected in ice cores from glaciers, which trap material that falls out of the atmosphere. These volcanic strata are useful for putting a chronology on the history that is trapped in the layers of ice that accumulate on glaciers year after year.

164

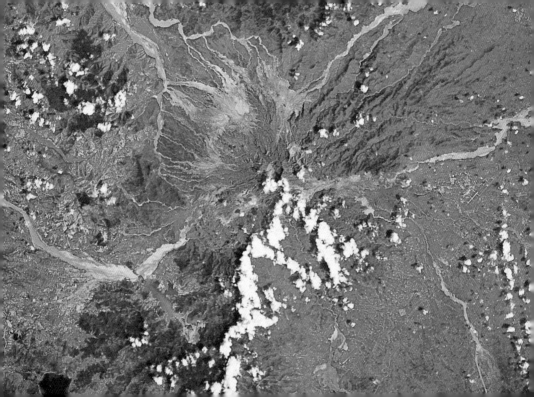

Australia

The smallest of the continents, Australia sits entirely in the Southern Hemisphere, with the Indian Ocean to the south and the Pacific to the east. The island continent has a landmass of nearly 7,665,751 sq km (2,948,366 sq mi), which is almost as large as the continental United States. With approximately 18 million people, the overall population density is less than 6 people per square mile. Much of the continent is desert, however, and the majority of the population lives along the coast. In this image, the lighter areas are major deserts: the Gibson and Great Sandy deserts in the upper left, and the Simpson Desert near the center. The city of Sydney is on the coast at lower right, Melbourne is at bottom right, and Perth is on the west coast. The island of Tasmania is just south of Melbourne. The Great Barrier Reef meanders through the Coral Sea, the waters in the upper right corner. The large inlet at the top is the Gulf of Carpentaria, with Cape York forming its eastern enclosure. Australia is known for its many unique plant and animal species, which have evolved and adapted to this isolated continent, including the kangaroo, the platypus, and the koala.

166

Lake Gairdner, South Australia

Lake Gairdner is located in the state of South Australia in a region that is very arid today, receiving less than 25 cm (10 inches) of rain annually. As a result of this aridity and high evaporation, salt flats (white areas) occupy a large portion of the lake basin. The lake is about 150 km (95 miles) long. North of this area, the catchment of Lake Eyre drains about 1,280,000 sq km (500,000 sq mi) of land. Many of the surrounding lakes form large salt pans similar to those along Lake Gairdner. During the Pleistocene, more than 10,000 years ago, there was a great deal more precipitation and runoff in this region, which washed large quantities of sand and salt into the lakes. Today the sand forms dunes in the Simpson Desert, which stretches northeast of Lake Eyre. To the southwest of Lake Gairdner in this image are the Gawler Ranges, which are covered by weathered lava flows. These are rounded hills less that 500 m (1,600 feet) high. The round basin southwest of the Gawler Ranges is Lake Acraman, which was formed by a meteorite impact 600 million years ago.

Lake Amadeus, Northern Territory

Lake Amadeus is located west of the Simpson Desert and Lake Eyre and southwest of Alice Springs in Australia's Northern Territory. It lies in a large sedimentary basin that extends east-west for 720 km (447 miles) and north-south for 260 km (161 miles). The basin is filled with a variety of sedimentary rocks. This is an intensely arid region. The combination of low precipitation levels and a high rate of evaporation increases the relative salinity of lakes in such regions. Extensive salt deposits result when these conditions are severe, as in Lake Amadeus (they appear white in this image). Lake Amadeus sits on the Western Plateau, which occupies more than half of the continent. Most of the plateau is 300 to 900 m (1,000 to 3,000 feet) above sea level. The highest elevation is on Mount Ziel (1,510 m/4,955 feet), located in the Macdonnell Ranges, which are just north of Lake Amadeus. Many of the salt lakes of Australia are located on the Western Plateau, which is characterized by topographic monotony and aridity.

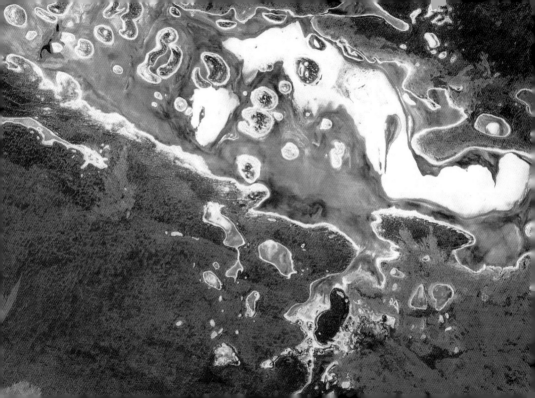

South Island, New Zealand

New Zealand lies in the South Pacific, about 1,600 km (1,000 miles) southeast of Australia. It is composed of two main islands—North and South—as well as Stewart, Chatham, and many small outlying islands. The landscape of the South Island of New Zealand is dominated by the Southern Alps, which formed by tectonic folding. The Alps claim the country's highest point, glacier-capped Mount Cook, which reaches 3,764 m (12,349 feet) in elevation. Numerous peaks rise above the permanent snowline, providing ideal conditions for the growth of glaciers, many of which can be found in the high-peak area around Mount Cook, north of this image. During the last ice age, more than 10,000 years ago, these glaciers were more extensive and reached the Canterbury Plains on the east coast and covered a large part of the Otago province in the south. Numerous lakes formed in these valleys following glacial retreat, including Lakes Pukaki (center), Ohau (left), and Tekapo (right).

Auckland, New Zealand

New Zealand's North Island is occupied by more than 70 percent of the country's 3.2 million inhabitants. The Auckland metropolitan area, which appears in the center of this image, has a population of about 1 million. The economy of the North Island is more diversified than that of the South Island, where agriculture is the main economic activity. There are major manufacturing facilities located in the urban centers of the North Island, including Auckland, which is also the most important port in New Zealand for international shipping. Many trans-Pacific ships stop at Auckland en route between Sydney, Australia, and North American ports. Auckland occupies an isthmus with a deep-water port on the east and a shallow-water port on the west, which can be seen just south of the city. An extinct volcano is visible just north of the city offshore. The North Island is composed of fold mountains and is dotted with volcanoes, some of which remain active. Roughly 100 years of logging has converted much of the landscape to pastureland.

Lakes Wanaka and Hawea, New Zealand

Lakes Wanaka (left) and Hawea are located on the South Island of New Zealand, in the Southern Alps. The lakes occupy large U-shaped valleys that are indicative of a landscape that has been modified by glaciers. There are still small glaciers on the island, although none appears in this image. Glaciers expanded in the past because of colder and wetter conditions, which resulted in greater snow accumulation, less melting, and hence glacier growth. Over the last 2 million years of Earth's history, there have been at least 20 major periods when glaciers around the globe have expanded. These have included phases when large continental ice sheets stretched across North America and Eurasia. When glaciers retreat they leave characteristic landforms, including U-shaped valleys, that are evidence of their great erosive power. Within these valleys, lakes such as Wanaka and Hawea formed when a basin was created by recessional moraines and trapped the drainage from higher elevations. The patchwork of fields at the southern ends of the lakes indicates agricultural activity.

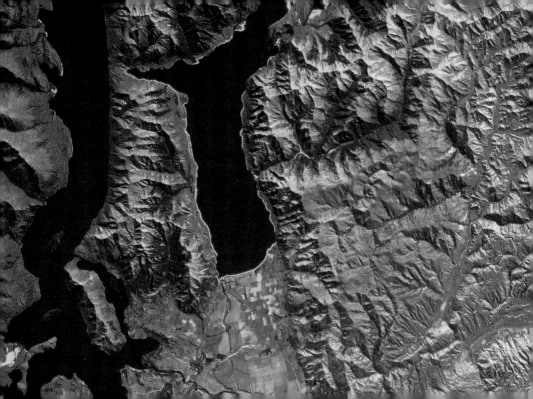

Antarctica

Antarctica, shown here in a color-enhanced mosaic image, is the world's highest, driest, windiest, and coldest continent, too cold for permanent human habitation. It is permanently covered by 14,300,000 sq km (5,500,000 sq mi) of glacial ice with a maximum thickness of 4,776 m (15,669 feet). More than 90 percent of Earth's fresh water is stored as glacial ice in Antarctica. In this photograph, the south pole lies below and slightly to the left of the apparent center of the continent, and the Greenwich meridian (0° longitude) is oriented toward the top. West Antarctica, to the left, stretches out into the Antarctic Peninsula, which points toward the tip of South America, 1,000 km (620 miles) to the north. The Transantarctic Mountains, which run from the upper left to lower center of the picture, separate it from East Antarctica (to the right). Also evident are two large ice shelves, the Ross Ice Shelf (the brownish-pink-tinted area in lower center) and the Ronne-Filchner Ice Shelf (the purple-tinted area above and to the left of center). These ice shelves are created as glacial ice flows into the Ross and Weddell seas, respectively.

178

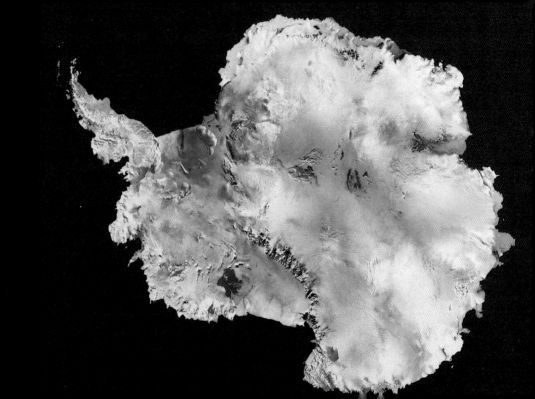

Palmer Land

This Landsat image from January 1973 pictures a portion of the so-called English Coast of the western side of the Antarctic Peninsula. In the lower right-hand corner is the continental mainland. Composed of floating glacial ice, the ice shelf that dominates the right side of the photograph lies above George VI Sound. Enclosed within the ice shelf are Spaatz Island and smaller DeAtley Island, visible in the lower left, and Alexander Island, at the top of the image. The lines visible in the middle of the ice shelf are fractures known as crevasses. The iceberg in the center of the photograph, which has only recently broken off from the ice shelf, is 35 km (22 miles) long. It is typical of Antarctic tabular icebergs, whose flat shape differs from the lumpy, irregular icebergs produced in the Arctic. Calving (detaching) of icebergs, as opposed to glacial melting, is the dominant mode of ablation, or glacial loss, in this supercold environment. The black, open-water region on the left is called the Ronne Entrance. It is a polynya, an area swept free of sea ice by strong winds.

Queen Maud Land

Queen Maud Land, on the East Antarctic coast, is shown in this 1975 Landsat image. Right of center is the Jutulstraaumen Glacier, one of the innumerable glaciers of the ice sheet that covers Antarctica. (In total, the Antarctic ice sheet covers an area of 14,000,000 sq km/5,460,000 sq mi, 1.5 times the size of the United States, including Alaska.) The direction of ice flow is from the bottom of the photograph to the top. The curvilinear striping is assumed to correspond with flow lines within the glacier, where neighboring streams of ice are capable of moving at different speeds. At the top center are deep cracks, or crevasses, which form when the ice is under tension. Jagged outcrops of the Fimbulheimen Mountains are visible in the lower right-hand corner. Isolated mountain peaks poking up out of the glacial ice are known as nunataks, a word borrowed from the language of the Inuit of Greenland, where the same phenomenon occurs.

West Antarctic Ice Sheet

This photograph was taken from the space shuttle in September 1991, at the beginning of the Antarctic spring. It shows the breakup of ice at the periphery of the West Antarctic ice sheet, a seasonal phenomenon. Offshore winds force the ice floes into the ribbonlike patterns visible in the photograph. Both large icebergs and slushy sea ice can be seen. Sea ice, frozen ocean water, has an average thickness of only 2 m (6.5 feet), unlike the kilometers-thick glacial ice. The extent of the sea ice varies from a minimum of about 3,000,000 sq km (1,160,000 sq mi) in the polar summer to a maximum of 20,000,000 sq km (7,700,000 sq mi) in the late winter, in effect doubling the area of Antarctica. The sea ice has significant influence on Antarctica's biologic, oceanographic, and climatic systems because it hosts flourishing microbial communities of algae and bacteria and plays an important role in regulating ocean-atmosphere heat and gas exchange.

Plate Tectonics

Earth's crust is broken up into about a dozen pieces, which are called tectonic plates. These plates are in constant motion, converging, diverging, and sliding past one another, as described in the introductory essay "Plate Tectonics." The plates form the ocean floors and support the continental landmasses.

The world map on the facing page shows the seven continents and the major tectonic plates. The white lines indicate plate boundaries. The boundary between the Pacific and American plates along the west coast of the United States forms the San Andreas Fault. The boundary extending the length of the Atlantic Ocean between the American Plate and the African and Eurasian plates is the Mid-Atlantic Ridge.

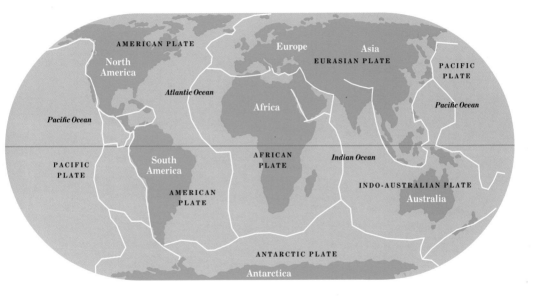

Index

Credits

Photographers

CNES/Spot Image/Explorer/Photo Researchers, 171, 175, 177
CNES/Spot Image/Explorer/Science Source/Photo Researchers, 103, 109
Earth Satellite Corp./SPL/Photo Researchers, 43, 45, 49, 53 (left and right), 61, 67, 69, 77, 79, 93, 107, 113, 117, 119, 131, 143, 149, 153, 159, 167, 169
Dr. Lene Feldman, NASA GSFC/SPL/Photo Researchers, 35
Geospace/SPL/Photo Researchers, 83, 87, 95, 97, 99, 101, 105, 111, 123, 151
Johnson Space Center, 73, 91, 173
B. Lucchitia/U.S. Geological Survey/SPL/Photo Researchers, 183
NASA, 57, 115, 141
NASA/Science Source/Photo Researchers, 33, 39, 47, 51, 59, 75, 81, 125, 127, 135, 157, 185
NASA/SPL/Photo Researchers, 37, 121, 129, 137, 139, 147, 155, 165
National Snow & Ice Data Center/SPL/Photo Researchers, 63, 85
Nigel Press Association/Photo Researchers, 133
NRSC LTD./SPL/Photo Researchers, 27, 71, 145, 179
RESTEC, JAPAN/SPL/Photo Researchers, 161, 163
U.S. Geological Survey/Science Source/Photo Researchers, 181

Tom Van Sant/Geosphere Project/SPL/Photo Researchers, 29, 31, 65
Worldsat International/NRSC/SPL/Photo Researchers, 89
Worldsat International/SPL/Photo Researchers, 41, 55

Cover photograph: Eurasia, Geospace/SPL/Photo Researchers

Title page: Sinai Peninsula, NASA

Page 20: Globes top row, *left:* NASA/Science Source/Photo Researchers; *center and right:* Tom Van Sant/Geosphere Project/SPL/Photo Researchers. Globes bottom row, *left, center, and right:* Tom Van Sant/Geosphere Project/SPL/Photo Researchers.

Page 21: Globes top row, *left:* NRSC LTD./Photo Researchers; *center:* Tom Van Sant/Geosphere Project/SPL/Photo Researchers; *right:* European Space Agency, colored by John Wells/Photo Researchers. Globes bottom row, *left and right:* Tom Van Sant/Geosphere Project/SPL/Photo Researchers; *center:* Geospace/SPL/Photo Researchers.

Pages 24–25: Flat Earth, Tom Van Sant/Geosphere Project/SPL/Photo Researchers

This book was created by Chanticleer Press. All editorial inquiries should be addressed to:
Chanticleer Press
568 Broadway, #1005A
New York, NY 10012
(212) 941-1522

To purchase this book, or other National Audubon Society illustrated nature books, please contact:
Alfred A. Knopf, Inc.
201 East 50th Street
New York, NY 10022
(800) 733-3000

Chanticleer Press Staff

Publisher: Andrew Stewart
Managing Editor: Edie Locke
Art Director: Amanda Wilson
Production Manager: Susan Schoenfeld
Photo Editor: Giema Tsakuginow
Photo Assistant: Consuelo Tiffany Lee
Publishing Assistant: Alicia Mills
Project Editor: Amy K. Hughes
Natural Science Consultant: Richard Keen
Maps and illustrations: Acme Design
Original series design by Massimo Vignelli

Founding Publisher: Paul Steiner